MALATHI
RAMACHANDRAN

MANDU

The Romance of Roopmati and Baz Bahadur

olive turtle

NIYOGI BOOKS

Published by
NIYOGI BOOKS
Block D, Building No. 77,
Okhla Industrial Area, Phase-I,
New Delhi-110 020, INDIA
Tel: 91-11-26816301, 26818960
Email: niyogibooks@gmail.com
Website: www.niyogibooksindia.com

Editor: Keerti Ramachandra
Cover Design: Misha Oberoi
Inner Layout: Nabanita Das

ISBN: 978-93-89136-54-8
Publication: 2020

This is a work of fiction. The names, characters and incidents portrayed in it are the work of the author's imagination. Any resemblance to actual persons, living or dead, events or localities, is entirely coincidental.

Printed at: Niyogi Offset Pvt. Ltd., New Delhi, India

Long after thy pavilions crumble down,
When age-forgotten Mandu's dying fame,
When Rewa's godhead, desecrate, departs,
Still shall thy songs be sung by sage and clown,
And green, as Malwa's monsoon hills, thy name
Live on her children's tongues and in their hearts.

From Lady of the Lotus,

By

Ahmad-ul-Umari

(Translated from the Persian by L.M. Crump)

for
Aria

Prologue

'If there is a book that you want to read, but it hasn't been written yet, you must be the one to write it.' Nobel Laureate Toni Morrison's words resonate with my own thoughts. As a travel enthusiast who often takes the narrow road, I have come upon stories that fascinate and intrigue me. History, legend, folklore ... these tales are born of events that once happened, or may never have, but we can sense them like ghosts flitting between the pillars of crumbling palaces, hear them like half whispers echoing in the depths of step wells. They lisp through the lips of the ancient and sing through the ballads of minstrels.

The legend of Roopmati and Baz Bahadur is a part of the very consciousness of Malwa ... a story sung by women as they work in the fields or winnow their grain. Roopmati to them, even today, remains the ideal woman, beautiful, gifted and pure of heart.

In the abandoned fortress city of Mandu, perched on the Malwa plateau, one can visualise how this vast complex of palaces and lakes would have looked 450 years ago. How its markets and gaming houses would have hummed with noise, and the zananas with song and dance. I knew I had to recreate it. To know what made a Sultan forget his kingdom for his lady, and his lady to forgo the world for him. To explore the nuances of power in Akbar's court and to imagine the game plan that brought the Mughal forces to the doorstep of Mandu.

And that is just what I have done. This, the story of Sultan Baz Bahadur and Roopmati is my offering to every reader who loves to be whisked away to another era and live other lives between the covers of a book. Welcome to Mandu!

Chapter 1

***When** the rains come to Malwa, it is as if the slopes and valleys and the river begin decking themselves up for wedding festivities. The hills preen in their green satin skirts and lilac chiffon veils that float around their peaks. The valleys choose their trinkets from the colourful gems strewn all over the meadows, reds and golds and greens and mauves. The forests cluster together like maidens huddling to gossip, their whispers lost in the clamour of calling birds and rustling breezes. And the Narmada, the sensuous, captivating river of the plains, she needs no adornment, but will not listen. For she knows she will always be the bride, no matter who her suitor. She sweeps gracefully down from the East, her curves so innocuous, and yet so voluptuous, her rapids so smooth and their sounds so melodious. And as the raindrops begin to fall on her waters, they turn into a million tiny diamonds falling into necklaces of pearls. And she, vain as the next woman, is happy at last.*

They say, when the rains come to Malwa, all nature celebrates. But it is also true that sometimes, a voice, a laugh, a song carries on the chameli-fragrant air and then the river and the forests wait with bated breath, knowing that history is about to be created here yet again, in the land of the warriors, their chattels and their citadels.

Baz pulled his horse's reins in and listened. But all he heard was the snorting of the horse, the jingle of its bridle and the patter of rain on the leaves above. Had he caught a lilt of a song on the air or was it just the sighing wind? He laughed and flicked the reins to move on. Sometimes he felt that his love of music had seeped into his mind and his body so much that he heard little else.

There it was again. A snatch of a melody on the monsoon laden breezes blowing from the river. Baz turned his horse's head towards the river, gently nudged his heels into its flanks and began to canter through the thick copse of trees. His two guards followed hurriedly on their horses. As he emerged onto the grassy banks of the Narmada, Baz drew in his reins sharply and the horse stopped and tossed its head, stamping restlessly. In front of him was the most captivating, colourful scene he had witnessed in days. Seven or eight young maidens were engaged in clapping and dancing together, their long tresses open and flying about. A few others were trying in vain to throw a rope over the branch of a tree, probably to create a swing. There was some bawdy humour, some bad singing and plenty of raucous laughter. Then one of them caught sight of Baz and his men. With a dramatic shriek, she pointed to them. All the girls looked around, nudged each other and lifting the hem of their skirts, began to run away, their laughter and excited chatter wafting back in waves.

Baz watched them with an amused smile and turned to leave. Then he froze. The song that had drawn him was back. He looked around, puzzled. Who was singing and where was the singer on this deserted bank of the river? The voice and the notes were irresistible.

Baz walked along the gushing river, led by the sound that grew louder and louder. At last, he came to a large, spreading tree and stopped. Below the leafy canopy sat a young woman, her face lifted towards the river. Her eyes were closed in ecstasy as she drew out the *alaap*, the opening notes, of Raga Megh Malhar. There was no drone of the tanpura to accompany her voice, but it was not necessary. The cadence, the pitch, the tempo were impeccable.

Megh Malhar, the song of the monsoon, a paean to the rain gods ...

In a dreamlike state, Baz sat down facing her. She completed the *alaap* and moved into the main raga. And as if it was the most natural thing in the world, Baz began to sing with her. Their voices rose together, taking along the intricate footwork of notes, rising and falling as one. His eyes never left her face and hers never opened.

As the song reached a crescendo, it was as if he could hear a tabla keeping pace. Then he realised that the rain had started falling hard, hitting the ground and rocks around, like a percussionist trying his best to make the *gati, the* beat, worthy of the vocal rendition.

Finally, the notes died away and only the rain was there, drenching them as they sat on the grassy bank. The maiden opened her eyes and looked at Baz for a long moment. Then she smiled, a gamine-like yet guileless smile that broke the spell.

'You are very wet.'

He stared at her in amazement.

'You seem unsurprised to see me. Did you not hear me sing with you? And did you not wonder who it was?'

She shook her head simply. 'No, because I thought my guru had come back to sing with me.'

'Your guru? Where is he?'

'He is no more with us. But his ashes were immersed in the river. So whenever I sing here, I know he is listening to me.'

Baz had no idea what to say to that. He felt as if he was with a *jal pari*, a water nymph, someone not quite of this world.

She gave a lilting laugh.

'Come, I will take you home. You can dry yourself and *Baba* will give you some hot masala chai.'

She jumped up and began to run on light feet, looking back teasingly.

'Come on, come on, you'll get more and more wet if you don't hurry!'

Baz began to follow her blindly. He had no clue where he was, where she was taking him, and whether he would ever go back to wherever it was he had come from.

~

She ducked into the low doorway of a small dwelling set back from a vast fenced-in field where cattle grazed. Inside, it was dark and smelt faintly of old age, sweet and musty, and a little like ghee gone rancid. As his eyes got used to the dimness, Baz saw a longish room with thick wooden pillars holding up the rafters of a sturdy roof. There was a rush mat along one wall with bolsters to lean on, and on the opposite side, another mat where a figure lay curled.

'My *dadi*,' the girl nodded in that direction with a softening of her tone, then called, '*Baba*! Where are you? Come out! I have a guest for you!'

A cotton drape at the far doorway was pushed aside and a man emerged, wiping his hands on a towel. He was plump and balding and grey-stubbled, and dressed in a farmer's garb of white dhoti and long kurta. Seeing the newcomer, he smiled and bowed, bringing his palms together in a namaste.

'Please come, come, you are most welcome in my humble home,' he said. 'I see the rain has not been kind to you. Please sit, sit, I will bring you a hot decoction made of herbs to drink.'

Baz laughed self-effacingly and looked down at himself.

'I better not sit. Your mat will get wet too.' He looked around for the sprite, but true to the nature of those creatures, she seemed to have disappeared.

'Oh no, no! Our humble home ... please sit, we are honoured.'

The man turned to go back to the kitchen, then stopped short.

'Oh my child, my child! You have brought the chai yourself!'

Baz turned towards the inner doorway, and then froze as his eyes fell upon the most beautiful woman he had ever seen in his life. His eyes lingered on her face, moving from her damp hair plaited back but still clinging to her forehead and cheeks in wet tendrils, to her eyes, large and thick lashed and dancing with laughter, to smooth curving cheeks and a full red mouth. His gaze slipped down over creamy bare shoulders to take in the attire that she must have quickly changed into. The green cotton cloth of the *neevi* fell to her feet in uneven folds, a black *asana* carelessly knotted around the hips. His eyes crept up again and lingered on the coarse red *kanchuki* tied around her breasts. Seeing his stare, the maiden pulled her cotton stole closer around her shoulders. He broke his stare and looked up as she approached him.

'Chai?' She handed him a brass tumbler, holding it by its rim, and held out a rough woven towel with the other hand. He accepted both and wrapped the cloth around the hot vessel.

How did I not see her like this when we sat next to the river? Was her singing so beautiful that I became blind for a while and could only hear her music?

He handed the empty cup back to the girl and dabbed at his head and face with the towel. As soon as the girl left the room, he turned to the old man with barely suppressed urgency.

'Your daughter, she is an accomplished singer!'

The man nodded slowly and thoughtfully.

'Yes,' he said, 'she has studied for many years under a great guru. And moreover, music is not a pastime for her. It is her life.'

Baz continued wiping his face. Then on a sudden whim, he decided to speak out a thought that had begun to writhe and rise within him. He threw away the towel and pulled himself up to his full height. Placing his hands on his hips in his characteristic stance, he looked down at the other man.

'I am Miyan Bayazid Baz Bahadur Khan, Sultan of Malwa.'

The old peasant cringed as if he had been physically attacked. He sank to his knees and clasped his trembling hands. He spoke to the Sultan's feet.

'*Huzoor*! Please, please forgive me! I did not recognise you. I beg forgiveness on behalf of my daughter and myself for any lapses in our speech or manners!'

Baz laughed aloud and shook his head.

'No, no, on the contrary, your hospitality has been warm and your deportment respectful. It is not of your manners that I am about to speak to you, but of your daughter!'

The man's bowed shoulders visibly tensed. He buried his face in his hands and waited.

'What is your name, my good man?'

'Thakur Thaan Singh, *Huzoor*. I own a small *zamindari*, growing paddy and grazing cattle for milk. We have lived on the banks of the Narmada for generations. Roopmati is my only child and I have brought her up ever since her mother died in childbirth.' He pointed to the prone figure on the mat. 'That is my mother. She remembers nothing, not even to eat or bathe any more. I take care of them both, my two children.' He stopped and waited in trepidation for the Sultan's orders.

Baz gave a short bark of laughter, of victory and anticipation.

'Roopmati! It is a name as beautiful as the maiden. I have a proposal for you, Thaan Singh. Roopmati shall accompany me to my fortress of Mandu where she shall be spoilt with silks and gold and silver and gemstones and live the life of a queen and give me the pleasure of her company.'

Thaan Singh clasped his hands together and bowed his head over them.

'Forgive me ... forgive me, *Huzoor*.'

'What is there to beg forgiveness for, *Baba*?' The cool voice cut into the old man's stammering protest.

Baz watched as Roopmati walked through the inner doorway towards him. Even as his eyes admired her beauty and grace, he could not help but notice that those doe eyes that had laughed mischievously at him a few moments ago were now narrowed with anger. She stopped in front of him and shook her head slowly, lips tightening with disdain. But when she spoke, her voice was as polite as ever.

'*Huzoor,* I thank you for your kind offer, but I cannot accept.'

'Why not?'

'I ... I cannot come to live with you, because ...' She hesitated for only a breath. 'I am already betrothed.'

'Betrothed! Is this true, Thaan Singh?'

'Yes, *Huzoor.* Roopmati is betrothed to Rann Singh Choudhary of Chanderi. But a marriage date has not been finalised.' He hung his head.

Baz waited for him to continue.

'Roopmati will not go to live in any place where she cannot see the river every day.'

Baz turned to the maiden. She looked away, as if the very sight of him was annoying to her.

'What is so special about this river?' he asked.

There was a long silence. Then Thaan Singh spoke again, softly.

'When Roopmati was a child, she once asked me where her mother was. I told her that the Narmada is her mother. Ever since then, not a day passes that she does not sit by its banks to sing, or to converse with the rushing waters. The river flows not just on the earth, but in her veins too.'

He joined his hands, pleading understanding.

'Please forgive me, *Huzoor*. And forgive my child. She cannot do as you desire.'

Chapter 2

As Baz turned the last curve of the hill and his horse nodded up the sweeping slope, the fort city of Mandavgarh shimmered out of the mist of fine raindrops like a maiden's face barely discernible through a gossamer veil. He finally pulled in his steed in front of the great fortifications of red stone that leaned back, guarding the secrets of life and strife that had played out within for centuries. The air was clear, more sweet and fragrant up here on the hillsides, and with the thunder of the river no longer in the ears, he could hear the rustle of trees sharing their own songs and stories.

Since he had left Thakur Thaan Singh's house, Baz's mind had been unable to dwell on anything but the beauty and the voice of the maiden he had just met. He felt a strong sense of having seen her before, but of course he hadn't. Or was it in his dreams that he had met her, when he would often roam the hills and forests, melancholic and lonely, yearning for the company of someone to share his life with? Perhaps she had always been there, in a snatch of music, in a pensive sigh, a presence he had sensed, but never seen. A soulmate that he had always yearned for.

Although he had his friends, the coterie of childhood playmates that he had grown up with, and his courtiers who fawned on him but kept a discreet distance, and indeed his harem of beautiful women, Baz had always felt a deep vacuum within, as if there was someone he still needed to meet who would understand him and his thoughts, his feelings, his longings.

And now perhaps I have found her ...

Baz took a deep breath, then looked around and up at the walls. At once, he forgot everything and his heart began to throb with a wonder that always accompanied his first sight of the fort city. His thoughts turned lyrical.

O Mandu! You were well named by my ancestors as Shadiabad, city of joy! For you are the haven of sultans and the abode of the blessed! I swell with pride to call you my paayah-e-takht ... where palaces and mosques rise gracefully around mirror lakes, where the forests and ravines echo to the call of bird and beast, where the sun comes home to roost in the waters at dusk, and the night stars pale before the brightness of a thousand lamps! O Mandu, may the silken ropes of your charm never loosen their hold on my heart!

As his horse stomped restlessly, Baz continued to drink in his first sight of Mandu. The thousand-year-old fortress sprawled on the Malwa plateau, the weight of her past sitting lightly on her. She had seen centuries of battles and conquests, perhaps the bloodiest during the Muslim invasions of the last three hundred years. It had all begun when Alauddin Khilji wrested Malwa from the Hindu Parmar Kings and made it a part of his Delhi Sultanate. Although the capital had then remained at Dhar in the plains, Mandu had become a favoured pleasure resort of all the rulers since, not least of them, Baz Bahadur himself, the present Sultan of Malwa.

Baz traced his ancestry to the dynasty of Sher Shah Suri, the Sultan from Delhi who, after conquering Bengal, had ridden to Agra with his armies to vanquish the Mughals, causing Humayun to flee to Sind. Then on a rampage of the Northern plains, he had easily taken Malwa and left his general Shujaat Khan to govern the state. Shujaat Khan made Sarangpur the capital and declared himself the independent ruler of the state. However, he did not live long to enjoy his power—he died in just seven years, leaving his territories to be shared by his three sons. Baz Bahadur, the eldest—Bayazid to his close ones—now sat on the throne of Malwa.

Baz grimaced at the flood of uneasy memories that rushed to his mind at the thought of his succession. Now was not the time for regrets and remorse. He kicked his horse's flanks and cantered towards the gateway, followed by his guards.

He entered the magnificent arched gateway between the row of liveried guards who withdrew their crossed spears and bowed deep. The city of Mandu rolled away to all sides, as far as the eye could see. The red stone-paved pathways branched towards parks, lakes, palaces and pleasure houses. Baz felt his mind calm down for the first time since he had left the old man's abode. This here, his beloved Mandu, was where he belonged, and where generations of sultans had retired to forget the cares of ruling over Malwa, the Sultanate that sat surrounded by the Mughals to the north, the Gujarat kingdom to the West and the Gond rulers to the South, like an enticing woman surrounded by lustful suitors.

To Baz, Mandu was more than home; it was a soothing balm to his spirit. Every time he left its pristine surroundings on a hunting expedition or a military campaign, there was little else that could draw him away. He always returned to his fortress home, hungry for its rolling, sprawling, grassy meadows, its crystal lakes reflecting azure skies and latticed green canopies, and its stately mahals that after dark would glow with lit sconces and ring with music and laughter. He had been away only twenty days, but coming home was as sweet as if he had been absent for months.

The fortress of Mandu, built within high stone walls, was flanked to the west and north by deep ravines and to the other sides by forests that sloped down to the Nimar plains where the Narmada flowed. The palaces, zananas, gaming arenas, bath houses and military barracks had been built by rulers over centuries and reflected their individual taste and style. The buildings had been created in the red granite of Malwa in a unique blend of Afghan, Persian and Hindu architectural styles.

To the north of the complex, lay the palaces of the Sultana and the nobles, all clustered around the lake Munj Talab, and across lay the Jahaz Mahal wherein lived the dancers, singers, and concubines. Nearby were the enormous step wells and their underground water tanks and secret passages, and the *hamam* or bath houses where the noblewomen were massaged with scented oils by handmaidens and sat in stone chambers heated by pipes carrying hot water as they waited to be bathed and dressed in their finery.

The pathways from these complexes wound south, past mosques and tombs and caravansarais towards a lush green oasis of silence only broken by birdcalls at the opposite end of the fortress. Here, the pond of Rewa Kund lay serene, reflecting the imposing palace of the Sultan, Baz Bahadur.

Baz reined in his horse at a fork in the bridle path and paused for a moment to look northwards towards the complex of mahals. Hiba had probably got wind of his return and would be waiting for him, decked up and ready with complaints and grouses to pour over his head. But even that was not as unpleasant as the thought of her mother, Jana Begum, deep voiced and chillingly hostile, her very body language accusing him of not being a good husband to her daughter.

Hiba had been the worst mistake of his life. She was the daughter of his father's cousin, a noble in Sher Shah Suri's court in Delhi. When Baz was just twenty, they had received an offer of marriage from Taheer Khan, describing his 14-year-old daughter as beautiful and competent in not just the classical arts, but also in horse riding, fencing and archery. A little surprised at so much accomplishment at such a young age, Shujaat Khan had accepted the proposal on his son's behalf and celebrated the marriage very soon after. On getting to know her however, Baz found her to be fresh and pretty, but shallow and petulant. After the first month's flush with romance and physical intimacies, he tried reading his poems to her, singing some of his compositions and discussing the nuances of his favourite raga Bhoop. But he soon realised that she had no interest in music or song, poetry or literature. Deeply disappointed, Baz began to turn more and more to the women of his harem, revelling in their adoration. Vacuous and fatuous though their attentions were, they satisfied not just his physical needs, but made him feel like a master of the arts.

When I am with Hiba, I am just a man, but with these beauties fawning on my every note, whether they understand music or not, I am a maestro.

He smiled with irony, then his thoughts came reluctantly back to his wife.

Over the years, his lack of interest in her had turned Hiba into a bitter, whining woman. In fact, as time passed, and he began to spend most nights in the arms of his concubines, he began to lose interest in visiting Hiba.

However, the hope of conceiving an heir would take him occasionally to her palace. But the very act of intimacy that had once given him pleasure, would become a chore, accompanied as it was, by Hiba's restless and discontented demeanour. Then he would tumble out of bed, mumbling some excuse about an early start the next morning, and ride back to his palace in relief. Now, even the thought of an heir could not interest Baz in seeking Hiba out.

Baz looked towards the Jal Mahal, the exquisite water palace where his Sultana lived, and shook his head. He turned his horse in the opposite direction and headed towards his own palace, his haven of peace, where he could be himself ... poet, musician and dreamer. Not husband, ruler or statesman.

The rain had stopped, but the breezes sprayed shivers of water droplets over him as he rode slowly below the trees, savouring every moment of the eventide in Mandu. And yet, his usual euphoria on returning home felt dimmed today;

there was an emptiness in him. That fleeting encounter with the maiden by the river had shown him that his life was hollow, meaningless. He may be Sultan Baz Bahadur, scion of the long line of conquerors of Malwa and ruler of all he surveyed, but deep inside, he was just a contemplative poet who needed someone to share his thoughts, his feelings, his craft with.

The horse skirted the tranquil Rewa Kund lake and came to stop quietly in front of the royal residence. With a sudden uplifting of spirits, Baz jumped off and ran up the flight of stone steps that led to the entrance. As he entered the courtyard, he saw Ahmed Khan in front of him, bowing low as he did *aadaab*.

'*As-salaam alaikum, Hukkum*,' he murmured.

'Ah! *Wah-alaikum salaam*, Ahmed!'

Baz smiled at his personal manservant indulgently.

'And tell me again, how do you always greet me just here, at this spot, so unfailingly?'

Ahmed folded his hands humbly in front and kept his eyes lowered.

'*Hukkum*, this is the magic of your own palace! As you know, *Hukkum*, any sound made in any courtyard or passage here is carried to every other corner of the mahal.'

'So are you implying that I made a lot of noise that perhaps disturbed you, while you were happily engaged in your own pursuits in your quarters?'

His bantering tone did not faze Ahmed. The man continued speaking in the same even tone.

'*Hukkum*, I was in your sleeping chamber, lighting the sconces for dusk, when I heard the sound of your boots on the steps.'

'Hmm! Next time I will test you, Ahmed, by removing my footwear when I climb the steps! Go now, and send me my masseurs with oil and *ubtan* and prepare my bath. I am weary and sore from hunting and travel.'

Baz burrowed his face into the cushion and let his body sink into the thick mattress as the two men began to massage him. They worked the warm perfumed oil over the corded muscles of his shoulders, into his arching back, and down his powerful legs.

He began to drift, his mind wandering into a twilight zone, and as always, the shadows and the phantom voices were back, coming up to whisper in his ears, only to be pushed away by another, only to be shouted down by another, and another ...

Baz groaned as they pressed the shoulder joint he had sprained while flinging a dagger into the body of a wild boar. He raised his head and looked around, bemused.

The *maalish* room was darkened with drapes and warmed by the glowing coals in an iron pan. A young boy plucked the strings of a wooden instrument unskillfully, making Baz's teeth grate. He raised a hand imperiously.

'Stop! That is enough of sound. He may leave.'

In the silence that ensued, broken only by the soft thuds and squelches of firm fingers and thick oil on hard muscle, Baz allowed himself to drift back into somnolent wakefulness, albeit pleasurable this time. He was on the banks of the river ... there was haunting music in his ears, a face drifted before him, but all he could remember was an enchanting voice and the rain on his face as he sang along in *jugalbandi*.

Roopmati. That is her name. What a perfect name for one so beautiful. Roopmati ... I want her in my life like I have never wanted anything else ever. Not my kingdom, nor my conquests, nor my Begum and not ever again, my harem of seductive women. All I want is her. To sing with, to hold in my arms, to spend the rest of my days with ...

Baz froze, holding his breath.

What did I just think?

You just spoke of making Roopmati your own.

Yes, that is what I want. That is what I will do.

But she is betrothed.

Betrothed, yes, but not willing to marry the man.

Yes, but that is only for one reason.

Reason? What reason?

Have you forgotten?

I have forgotten everything except her.

She will not marry the man because she cannot live where she cannot see her beloved river anymore.

River? You mean the Narmada?

Yes.

~

On a sudden hunch Baz heaved himself to a sitting position, his aches forgotten. He snapped his fingers impatiently and two boys hurried forward with a cotton robe. They wrapped it around him as he stood up, his form tall and formidable in the dim light. Within seconds, the men and the boys had disappeared and Ahmed stood in front of him with an apologetic cough.

'Will *Hukkum* take a hot, rose scented bath now?' he asked, his voice a whisper of velvet drapes.

Baz was already striding along the corridors skirting the chambers and out into the huge open courtyard. The evening sky was still streaked with colour, while a pale sliver of moon had already made its tentative appearance on the horizon. The pool of water that took up most of the courtyard trembled in the breeze. He paused among the marble statues that stood along the walls, women frozen in joyous dance or serene melancholy, and of men, belligerent, martial, victorious.

Arms on hips, Baz stood among them, unconsciously as imposing a figure, as he looked up and beyond his palace towards the ramparts of the fort where the stone walls hugged a two storied structure as they skirted the south eastern corner of the fort city. His eyes sought the silhouette of a canopied pergola on the terrace. He nodded thoughtfully, then ran down the steps of the sunken garden and out, then up a gently rising slope to the two-storied structure whose terraced roof looked over the ramparts of the fort. He walked across the long cool hall and up the stone stairway leading to the pavilion at the southern end of the terrace.

There, standing between two pillars, he gazed beyond the fort's boundaries, down the steep slopes outside Mandavgarh, to the rolling plains below, to the merest glimmer catching the last of the sun's rays, a sinuous, sensuous ripple that suddenly held all the meaning in the world to him. The Narmada.

Chapter 3

For the last two hours, Roopmati had felt her throat closing with claustrophobia every now and then. She was not used to sitting in a palanquin enclosed by white silk drapes pinned firmly down to prevent anyone catching a glimpse of the person seated within. As the palki swayed rhythmically to the coordinated movement of the four men who carried it, she bit her lip and tried to shift her folded legs without disturbing the movement; it must be hard enough for these bearers to walk up the slopes with her weight.

The bright red and gold cushions behind and around her set her teeth on edge. She liked only the colours of the earth, soft greens, warm browns and brick reds, mellow mustard and burnt orange. This tiny space was not just ugly, but smelt strongly of rose oil. Roopmati held her breath and thought longingly of the scent of wet red mud near the river, of the grass being cropped by the cattle and the smell of the river as she thundered by.

Sweet smells, do not fill my senses. My mind and heart must be empty for the muse, for when the notes and beats pulse through the self, for everything else, there will be little use ...

In the little dwelling by the river, Roopmati had dipped her quill in ink repeatedly and written in *Nimadi,* etching the letters carefully on cotton fabric stretched over a smooth long plank of wood. Outside, it was an afternoon washed clean and hung out to dry in the timid sun just showing between the clouds. There was music everywhere. The world was the bleat of goats in the pasture and the music in her head; the call of the koel on the branches and the music in her head; the rush of the river nearby and the music in her head ...

Suddenly, the door was pushed open and her father walked in, looking pale and agitated. His head waggled on his neck as if he were a rag doll being worried by a dog.

'Roopmati my child, my child! They have come!'

'Who?' she asked absently, as she rubbed her cheek where the pointed end of the quill had poked her. She was used to her father's panic attacks; he was known to be thrown off balance even when his cows calved.

'The Sultan, the Sultan! He has come with a large entourage of his men. They are riding here on their horses and have brought a palanquin along! And ... and ...'

Roopmati studied his reddening face calmly.

'*Baba,* don't be distressed. No harm can come to us! After all, what have we done?'

'My child, my child, you cannot be unaware!'

'Of course, *Baba,* I remember that the Sultan had asked me to go live in his capital and sing at his court. And I had refused! When I said I could never live where I could not see the river every day, he had accepted my decision. And left!' Her gurgle of laughter was tinged with triumph. Then she sobered down, stood up and rested her cheek on his shoulder. She spoke softly, her eyes dreamy.

'*Baba*, I am never leaving you. And the Sultan is surely a good man, an honourable man; he could have forcibly taken me, but he respected my wishes.'

There was a loud banging at the door. Father and daughter froze and looked at it, their demeanour suddenly like that of a deer mesmerised by a hunter's drawn bow.

The door was pushed open and a uniformed guard elaborately bowed and stepped aside. Roopmati watched fascinated as the Sultan walked in, bending his head to duck into the low doorway. She had forgotten what he looked like. He was so tall, their living space with its thatched roof and pillars and rush mats and large windows seemed to have turned into a crowded cow shed. Feeling hemmed in, she sucked in a breath and dived for her stole, her *uttariya*, lying on the floor and quickly wrapped it around her shoulders.

Baz Bahadur stood in the centre of the room, arms on hips in his usual style and his eyes flicked around the room and fell on the writing material lying on a rush mat. He read the words, then looked at Roopmati, a strange expression in his eyes. She stared back at him silently, unsmilingly, her chest rising and falling, as she would at someone who had chased her goats with a stick or aimed a slingshot at a bird in the tree. The silence stretched until she could not hold his gaze any longer. She bent her head and murmured with an effort, 'Welcome to our humble home, *Huzoor*. Please take a seat. I will fetch you some chai.'

She turned to go in, but in two strides he was in front of her.

'I have not come to enjoy your hospitality. I have come to take you to Mandavgarh.'

She stood still, staring at his riding boots, fine black leather trimmed with red velvet and laced up with silk braid that ended in ivory beads.

'*Huzoor*, I have done myself a great wrong.' She looked up at him at last and her measured words were at odds with the disdain that flared in her eyes. 'I have wronged myself, because I misjudged you. When I told you that my condition to ever leave my home is only that I should be able to see my beloved river every day, you did not say anything more. In fact you left soon after. My mistake was in believing you, that you respected my wishes. And I thought that was perhaps, because you too are an artiste; you can understand feelings, you can sense another's pain.'

At the last few words, his expression changed. He pursed his lips and looked away, his head nodding slowly. When he looked at her again, his eyes had lost their smile. He ran a hand over his bearded jaw and spoke thoughtfully.

'Yes, I am an artiste too. A poet, a singer, a lover of music. As you are. That is why I appeal to you to understand what I have to say. That day, sitting by the river, to the *taal* of the drumming rain, we sang together, and it was beautiful. I knew then that our voices belonged together. I want to share my world with you, Roopmati. I want to hear you sing every day, not just the Megh Malhar in the monsoon, but the songs of spring and summer, the songs of *usha kaal* and *sandhya kaal*, of sadness and longing, and joy and fulfilment. I want to listen to you, I want to sing with you, I want to make you my muse and hold you in my life forever.'

Roopmati brought her eyebrows together in faint annoyance. Her lips tightened.

'Can you cage a singing bird? Do you not know that it will die soon?'

He shook his head slowly.

'No, I will not cage you, Roopmati. You will live like a queen in your own palace. You will roam in the forests and sit by the lakes. You will have all the freedom you desire. And all I will ever ask of you is to sing for me and with me, and to read your poetry to me,' he glanced at the writing log, 'and listen to my imperfect verses. I am an artist in quest of inspiration and something tells me that you are the one.'

She shook her head, eyes flashing in anger.

'You speak of all *you* want! You want me to listen to you sing, and to sing for you, to recite for you, to inspire you! But, *Huzoor*, what about what *I* want?'

There was a slight hush in the air, as if the listeners feared the Sultan's reaction, his wrath. But his gentle expression did not change.

'And what do you want, Roopmati?'

'I want to continue to live here, by my beloved river, with my father and grandmother, who need me so much!' Her voice shook with emotion, but she cleared her throat and controlled herself quickly.

Her father turned away and pressed his white cotton stole to his eyes, his shoulders shaking.

The Sultan glanced at Thaan Singh and the old woman on her mattress by the wall. 'Do not worry about them. They will be well compensated with money and comforts. Your father may visit you once a month. Arrangements will be made for his journey.'

Roopmati felt her chest tightening with a portent of defeat. She knew she had very nearly lost. But she would not give up without a fight; there was one last coin in her bag, something she knew she could hold up to the Sultan, something he could definitely not counter with an argument.

She threw her head back and looked him straight in the eye. '*Huzoor*, you have given me an answer for every argument I made. But there is still one condition you can never fulfil.'

At the thought of her river, of leaving its banks forever, she choked up; her eyes welled up and a tear rolled down unwittingly; she rubbed it away fiercely, leaving streaks of *kajal*. He watched her every action, then spoke in a low, husky voice.

'I promise to fulfil it.' She was startled at the short reply.

'How? You are ... it is ... I mean, Mandavgarh is so far away ...'

He smiled down at her grey-smudged eyes.

'You shall see your Narmada, your Rewa, your Mahati every day. I am a man of my word, Roopmati. Please trust me.'

She went to the open window and stood looking out for long moments, collecting her thoughts. Then she turned and her face was stern, her lower lip caught between her teeth.

'*Huzoor*, you say you are a man of your word. But that is again only your word! You say I must trust you, but I can do so only when I know you have kept your word, is it not?'

He waited.

'*Huzoor*, I am expected to leave my family, my home, my river, only believing what you say, that I will see the Narmada every day! Why should I believe you? What will you do, if I simply refuse to go with you and live in Mandavgarh? '

There was a gasp from Thaan Singh. She ignored it and continued to look at Baz Bahadur, her breathing ragged.

Baz smiled and bowed his head.

'Roopmati, I will ask you a question in turn. When I came here on that rainy day, you had said that the reason you will never go to live elsewhere is because you will not be able to see the Narmada. Now I am promising you the sight of the river every day from my fortress city. Can you refuse now? Can you go back on *your* word?'

Roopmati looked at him, confused. He had turned the tables so deftly on her. She tried to think of a reply, but her mind was clouded with too many emotions. Finally, she nodded slowly.

'I am a woman of my word too. I shall come with you, provided you fulfil my conditions.'

~

She felt the palki turn sharply, and holding on to the wooden frame with one hand, she unfastened a square of cloth near her elbow and raised it cautiously. Her eyes swept the valley far below, looking in vain for a sign of the river, but all she could see were dense forests along the slopes, now buried in mist, just the tufts of treetops showing like green islands on a white lake. The Sultan had brought her here on his word of honour. Roopmati felt a twist of disappointment, sharp and painful. Gently raised, and taught the simple values of trust and honesty, she had believed the Sultan when he told her what had seemed impossible. That she would see the Narmada every day from Mandu. She bit her lip as she felt a prickle of tears, then hastily blinked them away.

Baba *has always taught me to be strong. He made me believe in myself and my inner power. In my gift of music, my love of beauty. He taught me never to let anyone else decide how I feel. So I shall not let the Sultan's deceit affect me. Let me reach Mandavgarh, then I shall ask him for an explanation. If he has no satisfactory reply, I shall ask him to send me back with dignity. That is all.*

Comforted by her thoughts, Roopmati sat back and was about to drop the cloth curtain back, when she gasped and craned her neck to get a better view. The stone fortress emerged like a mirage from the mists, taking her breath away with its magnificence. She stayed like that, her fingers holding the silk drape, her eyes following the lines of the walls and the turrets beyond as they drew nearer and nearer. At last, a huge gateway came into view, and beyond it, a flight of roughly hewn steps leading to a second gate. As it was late afternoon and the walls were bathed in a golden light, she guessed that they were on the western or south western side. She could hear the clatter of horses' hooves as the riders in front went up the steps. She knew that the Sultan was the last of them, immediately in front of her. Then she felt the men heave the palki a little and begin to climb up the steps in unison. Thrown back against the cushions, she listened to the sound of horses behind her too, snorting and harrumphing as they came up.

Through the second archway, the ground began to level out. She felt a cool breeze through the opening and looked out. Grassy meadows rolled away to the edge of the forests and there was an exhilarating smell of salaki and tailapatra in the air. She refused to let her spirits rise to the cold nip in the air up here. Instead, she looked around with prosaic interest.

She was in Mandu at last. The capital of the Malwa Sultans, and home of the man who had brought her here on false promises. She mentally shook her head.

I am not one to tolerate lack of integrity in a man, especially not in a Sultan. I, Roopmati, will show the man that I will not be abducted from my home, from my life, on false promises.

Chapter 4

Hiba Rahima Sultana turned petulantly from the full length mirror to face her mother, Jana Begum. They were a study in contrast. Hiba was tall and slender, her pale long face framed by jet black hair as striking as Jana's round brown countenance with its curly silver locks reluctantly escaping from the severe black burkha she wore even in her private chambers. They were quite unlike each other in temperament too. Hiba was quick to laugh and talk, cry and complain; she was full of a nervous energy that like froth on lassi, kept her light and floating, but slowly dissipated like its bubbles, leaving her flat and lacklustre before the sun went down for the day. She had no lasting interest in anything, be it art or music, clothes or jewellery, girlish gossip or serious state affairs. Nothing, except one consuming obsession. Baz.

She now spoke in an irate, shrill voice.

'*Ammijaan*, please stop trying to get me more upset than I already am! So the Sultan has brought home another woman. I heard! I heard! But that is *all* she is, alright? Another woman!' She raised a smooth white arm to point far away. 'There is a harem full of women there, *Ammi*! The Jahaz Mahal is practically overflowing with beautiful women, but has that ever disturbed me? No! And why? Because they are all whores, picked by the Sultan like pretty horses and kept confined there in the hope that he would one day call for them, one by one, two by two, or who knows, even the whole shameless lot of them together!' She stopped to throw a quick glance into the mirror, pouting her lips, her fingers unconsciously lacing through her black curls. Then she turned back to her mother, her features contorted into a sulky look again.

'*Ammi*, do you know who I am? The Sultana! The only Begum of the Sultan Baz Bahadur of Malwa!'

Jana Begum continued to stare at her daughter's face in silence for a few moments. Then she slowly sat down adjusting the folds of her loose outer garment, and extracted a *paan daan* from its pocket. As her daughter watched in frustration, she cracked betel nuts with a silver nutcracker and shook out a pinch of *zafrani zarda* from a silken pouch onto two leaves of paan brushed with *kattha*, then folded them along with the betel pieces into a tight triangle and tucked it into her cheek.

Hiba slapped herself on the brow and cried out, 'Now what? You won't speak? You won't say anything? You come in here to tell me what I already know, then seeing me agitated, what do you do? Instead of soothing my feelings, you keep quiet! What kind of a mother are you?'

Jana Begum chewed ruminatively; then spoke slowly.

'A good mother, I can assure you.' She glanced around the large room with its ornate pillars and velvet drapes; then leaned forward and whispered, 'This one is different. I heard she has been brought here to be his *mehuvivat*, his artistic muse.'

Hiba grimaced in distaste.

'Muse? What do you mean?'

'Apparently she writes poetry, composes songs and also sings so well that the Sultan has brought her here to live in Mandu and entertain him.'

Hiba continued staring at her mother for a few long seconds, and then suddenly burst out laughing.

'Poetry! Music! Entertainment! Oh! *Ammi,* it is too amusing! Like those dancing girls!' She shook her head and lightly slapped her cheeks in affected remorse. 'No, no, I must not laugh, the poor girl must have needed to make a living. She is lucky to find her way to the Sultan's court instead of singing and dancing in some cheap house of entertainment for drunken men!' She began to brush her hair with one hand as her other hand fingered *ittar* bottles of exquisite shapes and coloured glass on her carved metal shelf. She turned to her mother, '*Ammi,* you had better leave now. You know, Baz does not like your presence in my chambers when he is around. It's been a long time since he came to meet me, so I must get ready; he may be here any time.'

Jana Begum stood up, still chewing slowly, then went up to a spittoon and spat viciously into it, spattering tiny red spots on the wall behind. She shook her head at her daughter on her way out.

'I doubt it.'

Hiba had been married to Baz when she was fourteen and he was twenty, the eldest of Sultan Shujaat Khan's three sons and the most attractive of them all. It was an uneasy marriage. Baz's interest in Hiba was limited to the time he spent with her in the conjugal bed; her interest in him was a desire to consume his attention, his time, and then more of his attention. She dressed to attract him, learned music to please him and wrote a few bad poems to impress him. But the result was always the same. He would laugh at her and ruffle her hair, for all the world as though she were his little sister!

When his response threw her into an angry fit, his eyes would grow distant and he would walk away quietly, leaving her ineffectual sputterings to die down in frustration.

Why does Baz have this effect on me? Why do I crave his love so much and he take mine so much for granted?

Hiba examined herself in the oval full length mirror with its gilt carved frame of curling vine leaves, flowers and birds. She knew she was not perfect, her face was too long and her nose too prominent, but with her flawless ivory skin, jet black waist length curls and slender frame, she had always drawn the admiring glances of other women. She sometimes wished other men could see her too, so that she could gauge from their reaction, just what Baz found wanting in her.

And may be, they would find me attractive, turn to look at me as I pass, may be even whistle softly under the breath. Then I would feel beautiful. Oh, how I wish for that quiet inner confidence that comes with physical beauty, the confidence that I need to win Baz over again.

Hiba raised a hand and pulled the silk tassel hanging near her. A bell chimed softly outside the chamber and her maidservant Nasira came running in.

'Huzoor!'

'My red lehenga and net dupatta.'

Nasi kept standing, staring at her mistress with a strange expression.

'Did you not hear me?' Hiba's voice rose.

'I am sorry, *Huzoor*. Please forgive me, I am foolish, I am deaf, dumb, useless.'

Hiba had already lost interest in her. She turned away and lifted the corner of a thick drape to look out at the indigo night aglow with palace lights around and starlight above.

'So Nasi, where has the new singing woman been housed? Is she in the Jahaz Mahal with the other women?'

'No, *Huzoor*.' Nasi's voice was low.

'Oh, so she is not young and beautiful, then?' Hiba dropped the curtain and turned to her maid with an arrogant smile. 'One of those fat and ugly singers, is it? Well, some of them do sing well, I have heard. Not my taste though. It is like watching a koel sing. What do you do with your eyes, eh? Close them?' She let out a shrill ripple of laughter.

Nasi laid out the lehenga and choli on a chair and the tiny tinsel *chamki*s sewn into the outfit caught the lights of the sconces on the walls.

'*Huzoor,* let me help you to undress.'

Hiba ignored her and continued talking.

'I heard the Sultan has brought her from the Nimar plains himself. So how is she? What is so special about her that my *shauhar* has taken the trouble to escort her himself? Eh, Nasi?'

Nasi stood looking down at the floor.

'I did not see her, *Huzoor*.'

'But you have been hearing things, have you not? As we all have. So tell me something about her! How does she look? What is her age? What was she wearing when she arrived?' She approached Nasi with narrowed eyes.

The maid picked up the lehenga and held it out.

'*Huzoor*, shall I help you?'

Hiba pointed a long finger at her.

'You say, she is not going to be living with the other women in Jahaz Mahal. So where has she been housed?'

Nasi's face was pale. 'At the Shahi Mahal, *Huzoor*.' It was barely above a whisper.

'The Shahi Mahal! The Shahi Mahal! Are you mad? That is where our royal guests stay.' Hiba's eyes were blazing with anger. She pointed a finger at Nasi and raised her voice to a shout.

'I am going to ask you one last question, and if you pretend not to know, or speak a lie, you will be thrown out of the city before morning. Where is my *shauhar* tonight? Where is Sultan Baz Bahadur?'

Nasi was trembling so much that the garment shook, setting off a dance of lights in her arms.

'In the Shahi Mahal, *Huzoor*. Please forgive me!' She sank to her knees.

Hiba's chest was rising and falling agitatedly. She pulled the lehenga out of her maid's hands and holding it down with one foot, ripped it up, again and again. Then she threw it over Nasi's head and screamed, 'Get out! And do not come back unless the Sultan asks to meet me. And whenever he does, tell him that I am dead!'

Chapter 5

Roopmati lay curled on the thick mattress covered with silk sheets that rustled with every movement and threatened to make her slip her off the cot. Sleep was far away, but not as far as home. In the dim room lit by wall brackets that had been turned down for the night, she imagined herself back at home. She was lying on a rush mat near the open window. The only sounds in the house were those of her grandmother's occasional moaning and her father's ceaseless snoring. But her ears were tuned to the sounds of the river beyond the pale, and beyond the grassy banks. The waters snaked past with a hushed *gush,* occasionally chattering over the shallow stones and sometimes bursting into a splash of mirth on a rock. Remembering, she gave a gurgle of laughter in her throat and then stilled herself, straining to hear those sounds here too. But the weight of the furnishings and the high ceiling deadened every sound except that of her own breathing. It was all very new and strange. This imposing palace, the servants, the carpets, the lamps. Each new sight and sound an onslaught on her senses. Utterly overwhelming.

Roopmati buried her face into the pillow and pulled the covers up to her ears. But she could not stop the parade of images that flitted continuously and relentlessly through her mind's eye ...

The swaying motion of the palki had steadied and taken on a gentle bounce as the land levelled out. She knew they had entered the imposing gates of the city and were probably negotiating the pathways to wherever it was that the Sultan wished her to stay. Roopmati felt a sense of dread and desolation at the thought that home was left far, far behind, and she was at the mercy of one man in his kingdom. She swallowed the feeling of panic rising in her throat and sat back, listening to the sound of horses' hooves cantering on stone, behind, in front and all around her.

Finally, the movements slowed down to a mere walk and then came to a standstill. The horses continued stomping, their deep snorts mingling with calls of *ruk ... ruk,* and creating confusion in her mind. She closed her eyes and waited, her palms clammy.

Then the palki was set gently on the ground, its drapes untied and thrown up over the top. She blinked rapidly in bemusement, seeing herself surrounded by the legs of horses and uniformed men. In front of her, leaning down, with his arm resting on the palki, was Sultan Baz Bahadur.

'Welcome to your new home, Roopmati,' he said and extended a hand to help her. In spite of her swimming head and thudding heart, she ignored his gesture and clambered out of the deep seat on her own. She sensed, rather than saw, his rueful smile. Swaying slightly, she tried to stand straight, and nodded to him with silent dignity.

Dusk was just setting in and she could barely discern the greying shape of the building in front of her. She followed the Sultan up the broad stone steps, through passages lit by wall torches, into a very large square room whose polished floor reflected blazing chandeliers and tall windows draped with heavy red velvet drapes. Rich woven *dhurrie*s created islands of colour on the marble expanse. He turned to her and all the servants melted away beyond the doors and pillars.

'Roopmati, this is the Shahi Mahal. This where our special guests stay. I have had it prepared for you. I hope you will be comfortable here. There are rooms where you can eat, sleep, relax or meet other women. This room we are standing in is your *baithak,* your hall of public audience where we shall hold our musical evenings. Your instruments have been specially polished and tuned for you and kept in this alcove here. Behind the palace are specially created gardens where you can sit or walk around, and a menagerie with our collection of birds, peacocks, monkeys and even a leopard cub for your amusement.'

'There are maidservants to serve you day and night, and a *hijra* to guard your entrance door. And yes, I have called for a very special companion for you,' he smiled. 'A charming, lovable little person, to ensure that you are never lonely here.'

She stared at his face, barely hearing what he was saying. His teeth were sparkling white but slightly crooked, giving him a rakish look when he smiled. She looked away hastily and her eyes fell on a small person standing next to her. She gave a start and involuntarily shrank back in shock.

Close to her legs, reaching just above her knees, there was a tiny woman, or was it a child? Roopmati looked again and realised that it *was* a full grown woman. She had never seen a dwarf at close quarters before, and as the Sultan continued speaking, surreptitiously studied her. The little body was perfect, as if the Creator had turned into a miniaturist for a short while, but the head was large, the face full sized, with big black kohl-rimmed eyes, a long nose with a silver nose ring and ears from which swung elaborate silver jewellery. She had the deep self-assured voice of an adult woman.

'*Aadaab.*'

Roopmati was too well bred to display any discomfort. She nodded her head and tried to smile.

'Namaste.'

Baz gave a short bark of laughter.

'So! Well, it is nice that you both have now met. I am sure you are going to be good company for each other. Roopmati, this is Sadiya. She is educated in Persian and Urdu literature, she is also well versed in all the arts and music, and will surely be very stimulating company for you.'

Roopmati gave a watery smile and bit her lip, wishing this strange day would end soon and she could just curl up somewhere alone. How she longed for solitude after these hours of bruising aloneness.

'Sadiya lives in her chamber at the back of this house, while the other women in your service will be just ten minutes away. Sadiya's only job is to be with you whenever you want her, morning, evening or night. You can talk to her about anything under the sun; she can discuss, argue, debate any topic. She can appreciate your music and even sing with you.' He stopped for effect, then added,'But I will myself be here most days to enjoy your music. After all, that is why I have brought you here, is it not?'

~

Is it?

Sitting on the bed, long after the Sultan and Sadiya had left her for the night with one maidservant who lay down on a mat in the corner and immediately fell asleep, Roopmati now asked herself the question, her mind swimming with trepidation.

Is it really why he has brought me here? What if the Sultan's intentions are different from what he had said? What if he is just another young man drunk with power who picks up any woman who catches his eye and brings here to Mandu? Is all the talk of music and art just a game, a ploy to get me into his chambers? Am I in fact, now another minion of his court who will have to bow to his every wish?

She shook her head.

No, no, that cannot be true! Why, did the Sultan not come and meet Baba and request him to send me to Mandu with him? Did he not say that I would only be asked to sing for him? If he wanted, he could have just dragged me onto his horse and galloped away like so many marauding rulers do. No, Baz Bahadur is not like any of them. He has brought me here on the strength of his word. And most importantly, he has promised that I will be able to see the Narmada from here everyday.

Roopmati sat up straight, her eyes wide with doubt.

But where is my Narmada? How can I see her? Can I see her from these windows?

She jumped down from the bed and ran to the ceiling-high window and pushed aside the heavy drape. She looked out and then stood stock still, the river completely wiped out of her mind.

The scene that met her eyes was no less than the magical sight of a celestial abode of the gods. It was as if the whole sky had emptied its treasure chest of stars onto the city of Mandu. Lights twinkled from every building, lining roof tops, flaring in windows, entwined in the branches of trees. They dipped and blurred and shook below as the breeze rippled the waters of the Munj Talab. There was laughter, chatter and music in the air.

Roopmati drew in her breath sharply, gasping when she had no more space left in her lungs.

Magical! This is how it must be in parlok! Like a festival of lights! Indeed it must be Diwali every night here in Mandu!

She went to the carved rosewood wardrobe and pulled out the cloth bag that contained her writing materials. She sank down on the floor below the window and leaning on the wall, began to compose a poem, her mind so full of words that she couldn't wait to put them down. It was only much, much later, when she had finished her composition and was lying down, that into her slowly sinking consciousness crept a thought, an unsettling unease.

Oh Narmada ... I have come far from you and can see no sign of you anywhere in this strange, yet enchanting land. I must do penance for abandoning you. Tomorrow, my mother, I promise you, I shall atone ...

Chapter 6

***Bayazid!** Bayazid! Where are you? Look what we have for you! Where are you, Bayazid?*

The 14-year-old sank further down into the tall grasses and hugging his been sitar *close to his chest, curled up on his side so that his brothers could not find him. Ear to the ground, he could feel the vibration of their stomping feet just a few* hath *away; he clenched his jaws and closed his eyes against the trickle of sweat rolling down his brow.*

He felt a familiar resentment burn in his chest. Why did Daulat and Mustafa tease him so much? After all, he was the eldest, and deserved some respect. He lay there panting softly, waiting for them to pounce on him and take his beloved musical instrument and toss it away and tumble on the ground with him. And then they were upon him, holding his face down in the soil and pummelling his back with their fists. He felt the wooden neck of the been *splinter. With a shriek, he fought their arms and legs and their mocking laughter in vain.*

'*Huzoor, huzoor!* Are you alright?'

Baz suddenly grew still and with his eyes still closed, sensed the crumpled silk sheets under his cheek, the bunched muscles of his shoulders and the dampness of his brow.

He took a deep breath and turned onto his back as nonchalantly as he could, and nodded his head slightly, eyes still closed.

'Just some pain in the shoulders and back, Ahmed. Nothing to be concerned about.' He opened his eyes and saw the man's dark silhouette against the star-lit sky outside the window.

'May I send the masseurs to attend to you, *Huzoor*?' His voice was deeply respectful, revealing not the slightest knowledge of his master's regular nightmares.

Baz waved a dismissing hand.

'No. You may go now. I need my rest.'

He waited for the man to melt away and then sat up with a deep shuddering breath.

Bad dreams about my youth and my brothers ... one dead now and the other estranged and exiled! How strange is it that they still come back to haunt me. Me, Sultan Baz Bahadur Khan, ruler of Malwa, doyen of music, master archer and skilled horseman! And yet not a night passes when I am not awakened from deep slumber by these recurring nightmares and portents of doom.

Baz got up and went over to the window and looked out, trying to calm himself. He thought of his father, Shujaat Khan and smiled. *Abbujaan* had been a great influence in his life. When the Sultan of Delhi, Sher Shah Suri attacked and captured Malwa over a decade back, Shujaat Khan had been a general in his army. Pleased with his valour, Sher Shah appointed him the Governor of Malwa. Soon, most of North India was thrown into chaos as Suri's armies charged the Mughals at their capital Agra, and the emperor, Humayun, fled to Sind with his family and troops. In the midst of all the turmoil, Shujaat declared himself the independent ruler of Malwa, with Mandu as his capital.

What a beautiful heritage Abbu *left behind for us! A Sultanate that stretches from the Kali Sindh to the Narmada, all the land that lies between the Vindhyas and the Aravallis, the fertile soil of the river valleys and the dense green forests rich in game and timber and honey. He divided, he disbursed, he delineated our legacies, but forgot to tell us not to fight over them.*

As the cool breezes played over his skin, Baz tried to think of his brothers without getting emotional. Daulat Khan and Mustafa Khan, although younger to him by a few years, had teased and bullied him from the time they were children. Built large and thickset to his own slight frame, they would chase him, wrest his precious flute or *been sitar* or notebook of couplets from his hands and beat him up for 'playing and singing like a girl'. He grew up first resenting their behaviour, then despising them for what they had become ... brash, arrogant and spoilt young men who laid claim to anything they believed was theirs. And each of them believed Mandu, and in fact, all of Malwa, was his and his alone. When their father died suddenly, Baz as the eldest inherited the largest portion of the sultanate. But he soon faced a wave of anger and resentment from his brothers.

Abbu *left Mandu and the Nimar Valley to me. But my brothers were not content to accept their own share. They left me no choice ...*

He remembered the slow building of conspiracy, the secret meetings, the plots, the plans that his spy network would report to him about, and finally, when alone one night in his palace courtyard, the flash of a dagger in the dark, the struggle to overpower his brothers, the grunts, the pants, the gasps, and finally the long-drawn out groan of the mortally wounded as a heavy body crashed to the ground. His dagger dripping with blood, Baz panted as Daulat hit the ground, arms flailing, convulsing wildly in his last moments. He looked around for Mustafa, but he had already run out into the dark night. Baz heard the neigh of a whipped horse and drumming of hooves on the hard earth gradually fading into the distance.

With one rebel out, Baz and his soldiers soon chased his other brother to his territory and beyond, all the way to the kingdom of Gondwana to the east of Malwa, but Mustafa had already sought the help of the ruler there and they managed to resist Baz and drove him back to Mandu, wounded and defeated.

Traumatised by all the fighting and killing, Baz came home to lick his wounds, finding solace in drinking, music and women. His kingdom was safe for the present. He soon immersed himself in a life of ease, spending night after night drinking, singing, dancing and bedding his concubines. Nights were not for sleeping anymore, for they only brought on the nightmares.

Standing at the window, still shaken by his bad dream, Baz gazed at the rolling lawns beyond his palace, now just grey shadows in the starlight. Beyond them, he could see the forests crouching together, hiding the dark shapes within that moved stealthily, setting off the booming cries of langurs, and the shrill calls of night birds. Here, near the southern ramparts of Mandu, it was all quiet, the stillness centred in the deep silence of the Rewa Kund and radiating to the structures around it. But if he were to leap onto his horse and ride up the path, towards the complex of palaces, as he often did, the tranquillity would suddenly transform into tumult in the brightness of lanterns swinging from trees and to the sounds of music and raucous laughter, the ringing of *ghungroo*s as hennaed feet struck the ground below swirling skirts, stepping nimbly between the coins being tossed on the polished floor.

He saw himself alighting from his horse and walking through the main entrance of Jahaz Mahal. As he entered the vast audience hall bright with lamps along its walls, the dancing women would stop to do *aadaab* with bejewelled hands, smiling provocatively, their kohl-lined eyes enticing him, even as the lounging men would scramble to their feet, hastily putting away their silver *paan daan*s and silk bags of coins. They would melt into the background as he lazily surveyed the young women through half-closed eyes, his hands on hips. The girls would giggle and titter, the bolder ones coming close, letting a hand brush his arm or a sheer silk dupatta slide away to reveal a tightly moulded choli that could barely hold the curves in. He would pull a girl to him, giving a victorious laugh at her excited gasp and saunter away with an arm around her waist, pulling another one along by the arm. He could hear the dramatic cries of disappointment from the rest and then, as the heavy velvet curtains fell behind him in the scented pavilion overhanging the lake, the sounds of music and *ghungroo*s would start again.

Or if in a lighter mood, he would clap his hands for a lively folk song, throw off his *chogha,* fasten pearl *ghungroo*s around his ankles and dance, turning and twirling to the enticing rhythm, while the girls would join him, and the men would cheer lustily, urging their Sultan on.

Baz visualised the Jahaz Mahal blazing like a ship on the night seas, its lights setting the waters of the Munj Talab on fire. Then his gaze went beyond the lake to its further bank, where the palaces lay. His mind lingered on the Shahi Mahal, where Roopmati was probably asleep now.

Roopmati. What was she, a sylph of the forests or just a seductress with a honey voice? A water nymph or just a beautiful woman ripe for the picking? He closed his eyes and saw long tresses cascading over curves to which the *kanchuki* and *asana* clung, making him long to unwrap them from around her, to find out how her body would feel, how her lips would taste, how he could play her senses to make her gasp for more.

He felt himself getting aroused and quickly changed his line of thought.

She will be another exquisite gem in the necklace of my beloved Mandu! I must remember that I brought her here to hear her sing, to sing with her, to be lost with her in the world of music and poetry ... that she is not a whore to be disrobed and enjoyed.

Why not?

Because she is ... different.

How different?

She is not one of those brazen women of my harem whose only desire is to be bedded by the Sultan and become his favourite mistress and have him cover her in silks and jewels.

So what is it about her that attracts you?

She's beautiful and gifted and honest. Nothing pretentious about her. And she's not interested in ... in things. No, she's an idealist like me.

You understand all this from the few times you have met her?

I do. I understand her. It is like I have known her all my life. In fact, known her from another life too.

He cupped his palms and raised them together to the Heavens to pledge solemnly.

'*Ya Allah* ... I hereby take a solemn oath that as I have brought Roopmati here to Mandu as my muse and singer, I will never force her to be anything to me other than that.'

He brushed his hands over his face and opened his eyes. For the first time in years, he felt his spirits lift at the thought of the morrow. He could not wait to ride down to Shahi Mahal to meet Roopmati again and hear her sing.

Then he looked up at the thin crescent of the moon high in the sky. A star twinkled bright within its curve. It seemed a portent, a prophecy, a promise.

Chapter 7

As Baz cantered along the path that meandered between lakes and forests, he looked around with new eyes and marvelled at the beauty of Mandu after a night of rain, as fresh and innocent as a maiden coming out of the *hamam ghar*, glowing with the effect of scented oils and warm herbal waters. The trees were vividly and almost obscenely in blossom. The monsoon cassia hung like bunches of yellow grapes, while blooms of multi-coloured hibiscus, wild rose and indigo elbowed each other, jealously conspiring to keep his eyes from wandering upwards to the magnificent canopy of burnt orange overhead. But the gulmohar was not to be outwitted thus; Baz looked up in delight every time the spreading boughs shook a shower of the damp flame coloured petals over him. He laughed low in his throat.

As if it has connived with the morning breeze to strew my path with promising omens.

The whole world looked as if it had just been reborn, not the least because he felt different himself. Twenty-two years of struggling with his inner self, and after that, four years of fighting his inner demons had left him with very little joy. Many a time, nights of drinking and debauchery had merged with days of excesses until unable to bear the cycle anymore, he would toss his cup aside, pick up his *been sitar,* caress its strings, and begin to sing. Then the same courtiers who had breathed stale air into his face as they shakily poured another drink into his goblet, would sink back onto the cushions and listen to his compositions as he sang in his own unique style. Then, *then,* Baz would feel alive again.

He skirted the Munj Talab, his eyes on the complex of palaces beyond. The morning sun fell on the red granite of the Shahi Mahal and turned it into a ruby-red jewel.

A jewel within the jewel. Cannot wait to hear Roopmati sing.

He jumped down from his horse and ran up the steps and into the passage that led to the large *baithak,* the hall of audience. Then he stopped, the hair on his arms bristling as he stood still, listening. He could hear the high note of a raga being held almost endlessly. Awed by the finesse of the singer, he waited until the notes came down, and then quietly entered the plushly appointed hall. Roopmati sat on the carpet, holding the tanpura close to her chest; her eyes closed as she remained deeply engrossed in her music. Baz stood watching, listening, emoting with the singer.

The morning sun coming in at the window fell directly on Roopmati, turning her hair to deep brown silk. Her skin glowed like the petal of a champa flower and Baz's eyes trailed down her body, her red *neevi* in soft mulmul clinging to her curves with the careless ease of a pepper vine on a tree trunk.

He stood, swaying slightly, his palms damp with feeling. He had forgotten his pledge of the night before. He had forgotten that this woman was to be nothing more than his muse and his singing partner. She was just a beautiful desirable woman whose voice he had fallen in love with. And now, he realised with a shock, that he had fallen in love with the woman too. The song ended, and it was as if the silence in the room was a reproach, a rebuke, for the thoughts running through his mind. She opened her eyes and studied him calmly.

'Namaste, *Huzoor.*'

In response, he hastily raised his fingertips towards his face.

'*Aadaab,* Roopmati. I hope you were comfortable last night? Did you sleep well?'

She continued to look at him in silence. A little unnerved, Baz went and sat down in front of her. Sadiya suddenly appeared from somewhere and placed a silken bolster behind his back with her tiny hands. Baz and Roopmati gazed at each other, his eyes eager and a little shy, hers bland and expressionless.

'Roopmati, let us sing Bhoop raga together. It is one of my favourites.'

She shook her head. 'I cannot sing with you, *Huzoor.*'

His eyebrows came together. He flicked a look at Sadiya and back at Roopmati.

'I don't understand. You are now my personal musician. All that is expected of you is to sing for me, and with me.'

She looked down at her hands silently.

Sadiya walked mincingly up to him on her little feet and spoke into his ear in her deep, womanly voice.

'*Huzoor,* Bibijaan has not had anything since she woke up, not even a drop of water.'

Baz turned back to Roopmati.

'Is this true? Is there anything lacking in my hospitality that you refuse to eat or drink?' His voice rose sharply.

She stayed silent, her eyes lowered. He shook his head slowly.

'So, this is your way of defying me, of protesting against being brought here?' Without another word, he stood up in his usual stance, arms akimbo, looking down at her.

'I did not expect this from you. I believed you to be a simple country maiden without any guile. A person who only spoke the truth, and who let only truth guide all her actions.' He paused, a moment heavy with disappointment. 'You may go back to your home, as it appears you do not believe in honouring your side of the agreement.'

Roopmati's eyes flashed as she looked straight at him. About to turn on his heel and walk away, he stood mesmerised by her large, limpid eyes.

'*Huzoor*, it is not I, but you, who have not honoured our agreement.'

He shook his head unbelievingly.

'*I* reneged on what I had promised? *How*? You have been brought here with all due respect, you have been treated not as a woman of the harem, but as an honoured guest, and I have personally seen to your comfort in this palace. I told you that you will only be here as a singer for my pleasure and the only demand made on you will be to write and compose songs and to hold *mehfils* with me and some women artistes of my court so that we may sing together and share our love for music.'

'I am deeply grateful to *Huzoor* for the honourable treatment meted out to me from the time I left my home. But you seem to have forgotten my condition for coming here to live in Mandu.' She paused and waited.

The faint arrogance in Baz's eyes gave way to a look of puzzlement, then lit up in an epiphany. He smiled and bit his lower lip as he nodded slowly.

'My apologies. You are right, of course. It is entirely my fault that I have forgotten the most important part of our agreement. I can only argue that it was my eagerness to hear you sing and to sing with you, to re-create those magical moments on the banks of the Narmada that made me forget the river itself! 'His cheeks creased in an audacious smile. 'When you see your river, you can convey my apologies to her yourself!'

Roopmati felt her heart begin to thump.

So he is going to take me where I can see the river? But how is it possible? We are here, high up in the hills with only forests around. How will he show me my beloved river? Oh Narmada Ma, please do not let this be a mockery of my devotion to you! Please, let me cast my eyes on your pure waters, they are already pining for a glimpse of you!

Without moving his eyes from hers, Baz raised a hand. There was a discreet step at the doorway far behind him.

'Bring the palki for Bibijaan.'

'Come, Roopmati. It is time to show you that the Sultans of Malwa may have been plunderers and ruthless rulers. But we do keep our promises.'

As Roopmati rose and walked to the door, his eyes followed her. Her hips moved with the unselfconscious grace of one who was not used to the assault of male eyes. Her long hair had come undone from its loose knot and cascaded down her back to sway in tandem with her body.

Yes we do keep our promises. So Allah help me to stay detached and not lose my senses in her.

Chapter 8

Sultana of Malwa, Hiba Rahima Begum lay in the massive four poster bed, watching the door through the white muslin curtains. She was not angry, she was furious; not hungry, but weak from a self-imposed fast, not ill, but sick with despair.

She had not eaten anything since the previous night. She had overturned the silver *thaal* of food Nasi had laid out for her on the low carved table, and banished her to her room, weeping into her *odhni*. She had then looked around for something else to vent her frustration on. By the time she had thrown herself wearily on her bed, the crescent moon was high overhead and the room resembled a cloth market that had been raided by a marauding army. Cushions and pillows were strewn around, fine muslin garments ripped to shreds, the sheer curtains around the bed yanked out of their hooks, and priceless *dhurries* kicked into corners.

Hiba pictured the maidservants cowering behind the door, wide-eyed and skittish, waiting for the smallest sound from within, that they may scurry in to attend to her. She watched the door, willing it to open, willing the Sultan to walk in, resplendent in his riding outfit, his deep red *chogha* fastened with brass buttons over fawn coloured leggings tucked into brown leather riding shoes. He would pause on seeing her hazy form through the muslin drapes, and then stride forward to part the curtains and pull her into his arms.

He would gaze into her face and smile his special, crooked smile and say. 'Is my *mallika-e-jigr* angry with someone? Tell me who it is, and I will fight him until he dies!'

She would swallow her giggles and mumble something under her breath.

'Oh, *him*?' he would exclaim theatrically, 'If he made my Hiba Begum so unhappy, then he shall surely be banished from Mandu!'

She would cover her face and break into helpless laughter, shaking her head.

'No, it is you! Oh Baz, it is you who made me so unhappy!'

He would feign shock and slap his brow and she would put out a hand to stop him.

'Baz, do you love someone else?' her voice would quaver. 'Am I not important to you anymore?'

He would lay her gently back on the pillows and put his head next to hers.

'You know you are the queen not just of my heart, but also of my body,' he would say softly, his hand slipping behind her back to untie the strings of her choli. Hiba closed her eyes and imagined how it would feel to have Baz to herself at last ... the warmth of his hands and lips, the weight of his body, the crispness of his beard. It had been so, so long, that she had almost forgotten how it felt like to make love ...

With an effort, she came back to the present and looked at the door again. Perhaps, if she gazed at it long enough, Allah would make her wishes come true.

The heavy door swung open and Hiba sat up abruptly, hand on thudding heart.

She watched as Jana Begum sauntered in blandly, her portly form in the burkha suddenly bringing a sense of mundanity into a chamber charged with emotion and drama.

Apparently insensitive to the mood she had walked in upon, she stopped at the spittoon and shot a jet of red into its sandy bed, then continued to Hiba's bedside, ignoring the turmoil in the room and on her daughter's face.

'Get up,' she barked. 'It is past mid-day.'

Hiba wrinkled her nose in distaste.

'I will not get up until Baz himself comes here to me!'

Jana Begum reached out and roughly pulled the drapes apart to let the light in.

'Then you are going to stay in this bed for the rest of your life!'

Hiba sat up, hair tousled and eyes a little wild.

'*Ammi*, I am warning you, do not speak to me like that! I ... I will not take any more scoldings from you. Uff! I have had enough!' Her lips trembled and her eyes began to well up.

Unfazed, Jana Begum walked around the room, kicking the scattered clothes out of the way. She opened a window and the air, warm and heavy with rain, wafted into the room, mingling with the smell of stale food and enclosed spaces.

'It is going to rain,' she remarked, conversationally, then turned towards the door and clapped her hands imperiously. The door opened very slowly and a head looked in timidly.

'Begum Saheba?'

Jana Begum swept a hand to indicate the room. Two maidservants quietly entered and began to pick up all the strewn items, then swept the floor and wiped the tables and walls splattered with food. Hiba sat silently, the fight gone out of her with hunger and weakness.

Finally, the two women left and two others walked in, carrying lace covered platters and jugs of juices and lassi. They arranged the plates and the fragrance emanating from the steaming hot food ... curried meats and vegetables and seasoned dal and tawa rotis smeared with fresh ghee ... made Hiba moan and bury her head in her hands.

'Go wash your face, then sit down and eat,' Jana Begum told her daughter. She settled down on one of the cushions next to the low table and opened her *paan daan*.

As Hiba ate, Jana Begum watched her expressionlessly, chewing on a roll of her favourite paan preparation even as she mechanically cut more betel nuts with the silver nut cracker. Finally, as if her patience had run out, she snapped the lid of the silver case shut and glared at her daughter.

'Sultana! Mallika! Malwa ki Shahzadi!' she sneered. 'Is that what you think you are? Arrey, you are not even a whore in the Sultan's harem. At least *those,*' she nodded in the direction of the Jahaz Mahal, 'he seeks out for a night! But you ... you are now out of his life! He does not need you! And do you know why? Because his whole life now is music. He cares for nothing but composing poetry and songs and music ... and singing! And you, you know nothing about music! To play a tanpura in front of you would be like ... like flying a kite! You would probably look up at the sky to see where the strings go!'

Now replete with food, Hiba sat silently, her eyes downcast. She was not interested in listening to a homily from her mother, but knew that it could be in her best interests after all.

Jana Begum chewed some more. Then she bent and picked up a spittoon from under the table and holding two fingers to her lips, spat deftly into it, then wiped her mouth carefully with a cloth.

'That woman, that ...' she jerked her head backwards, 'that singer from the Nimar plains, did you know that she is young, beautiful *and* a talented musician? He has brought her here ostensibly for her music, but they say he is very attracted to her. He was seen there last night, he was seen there first thing this morning, and they were seen going towards his palace after that, her palki following his horse!'

Once again Hiba's eyes began to fill up. She spoke bitterly.

'You know, you are a very cruel mother! You keep saying things to deliberately hurt my feelings!'

Jana Begum leaned forward.

'Beti, I have to break your heart gently so that the world does not break it hard! Now listen to me,' she glanced towards the door and quickly out of the window. 'You have been married to Baz Bahadur for over six years now. I never approved of the match, but your late father, close aide that he was of your husband's father, insisted and had his way. I always felt that Baz was not tough enough to be a ruler, but some years back, when he fought his brothers and won Malwa from them, I was glad. After all, you had become the Mallika and would rule over all the Malwa region! But my happiness was short lived. Ever since his humiliating defeat in Gondwana, he has become a wastrel, spending all his time either with music or in hunting, and with his fawning courtiers and his flattering courtesans! And what was the result?' She pointed a thick finger at her daughter. 'He forgot you. How many times has he come to you in the past one year?'

Hiba remained silent. Jana Begum nodded grimly and started counting on her fingers.

'He came here on *Id ka jashn* to wish you. That was two months back. Then he came here once before that, because you had a fainting spell one hot afternoon. Apparently, they told him you were with child. If he had had the sense to think that he had not slept here for over six months, he would not have been foolish enough to believe them!'

Hiba's face flushed as she tried to knot her tangled hair. She rose, shaking her head dismissively.

'*Ammi*, I don't know where all this is leading. I suggest you go back to your chambers and rest for some time, while I go and take a bath.'

Jana Begum remained sitting.

'Hiba, you have lost him.'

Hiba stopped and turned, stamped her foot in a sudden flash of spirit.

'I have not lost Baz! He is mine and will always be mine, no matter how many women drift in and out of his life!'

'Really? Then how is it that he has stopped coming to you as a husband should to a wife? And now with this singing woman here, seeing him every day, you will not stand a chance.' She paused and her eyes softened for the first time. She pointed to a seat in front of her. 'Sit down! I have a plan. Listen and do as I say.'

Chapter 9

Roopmati sank to the floor near the window of her *baithak*, folded her arms along the marble sill and with a deep sigh, brought her chin to rest on them. Dusk was beginning to transform the sky and the lake and the monuments around it from oil paintings in vivid hues into charcoal sketches softly buffed with a piece of mul. As the greys emerged, pale silver tones here, a pigeon wing shimmer there, the colours slowly dissipated into the waters of the lakes, leaving dark silhouettes watching over Mandu like sentinels of this witching hour. She drew in a long, ragged breath and sat in the twilight, quietly savouring this time before the first *peher* of the night, hoping in a corner of her mind that the sconces would not be lit just yet. She liked it here on the floor, gazing at the darkening world outside, in the silence of her thoughts and the music of her feelings.

My river ... I have seen her again. And the Sultan is not a trickster after all. He spoke the truth when he said that I would have darshan of the Narmada every single day here. That first morning, in this very hall, when I had confronted him about keeping his word, he had led me through the wooded bridle paths of Mandu, to show me that cherished sight.

The palki had followed his horse faithfully, wending its way between copses of flowering trees live with birdsong. They had passed lakes and fountains and monuments before Roopmati realised that they were going back along the same pathway that they had come the evening before. But at a fork in the trail where one path led back to the entrance gate, the horses took the other branch and clomped along steadily. She noticed that they seemed to be heading in the direction of the massive boundary wall bordering the south-eastern side of the city. Finally, at the base of a grass-covered mound, the entourage stopped and Baz dismounted. The palki was set down gently and Roopmati stepped out and looked around her wonderingly.

She saw that at the top of the mound was a long, pillared pavilion, whose terrace was almost level with the top of the city wall. Mystified, she followed Baz up the slope and into the pavilion. They walked along the cool, dark hallway to a stone stairway at the end. Climbing up, they came out on to a vast, wind-swept terrace with cupola-topped pavilions at either end.

Holding her stole whipped by the breeze close around her, Roopmati reached the pergola overlooking the wall and peered down. Far, far below lay the Nimar valley, chequered in shades of green and yellow, with the Vindhyas forming a hazy blue-grey fringe beyond. And then she saw it, the silver trickle of the river, flowing gracefully from the east. And her breath was snatched away with the breeze.

'Bibijaan?'

The soft yet thick tones of the voice brought her back to the present. She turned and saw a tiny figure hovering near the door.

'Panna wants to light the sconces in your chambers. It is late evening, Bibijaan.'

Roopmati sat silent, loath to let the flare of lamps take away the magic of the hour.

The voice softly continued, 'It is alright. I will tell him to wait until you call us,' And then melted away.

Roopmati got up and padded to the corner where her sarangi stood against the wall on a silk *dhurrie*. She picked it up, spread the mat near the window, sat down and began to play. The notes wafted softly at first, then as their richness and depth so evocative of a human voice built to a crescendo, expressing first the joy of the music, then the loneliness of coming to live in a place where there was neither love nor companionship, and then finally, the deep sadness of parting from her loved ones.

She forgot her surroundings and played until she and her instrument were one and the tears flowed from her closed eyes.

At last, exhausted with emotion, she stopped and opening her eyes, gazed wonderingly out of the window. Hundreds of lamps lit up the monuments and the trees as they had the evening before. The sight enthralled her. It seemed that she would never cease to be fascinated by the sight of Mandu in the night, no matter how many times she saw it. She heard a footfall and turned to see Baz in the room.

'Roopmati, does this sad music mean that you have not forgiven me yet?' There was a smile in his voice.

She shook her head in the semi darkness.

'There is nothing you have done wrong, *Huzoor*. In fact, I am deeply indebted to you for keeping your promise.'

'So, does it mean that we shall sing together at last? In that case, the people of Mandavgarh are going to be confused indeed.' He gave a soft laugh and swept a hand out. 'When you played just now, the lights came on all over Mandavgarh, but when I sing, they may all go out! If this goes on all evening, what is to become of our city?'

She smiled and at that moment, Sadiya walked into the hall with a lit torch in her hand. In the circle of light, Roopmati's eyes looked as wide and thick lashed as those of a deer shyly raising its head from the grass. Baz could not look away. He stood transfixed.

'Ah, *Huzoor*!' Sadiya's laughing voice broke the spell. 'Bibijaan's smile has lit up the room indeed!'

Baz turned towards her, tearing his eyes away from Roopmati's face. 'Yes, Sadiya, I was just telling her the same thing about her music.' With that remark, he started to walk away.

'*Huzoor*,' Roopmati's voice was a little hesitant. '*Huzoor*, I have one more question for you.'

'Yes?' He stopped.

'On a rainy day ... the river will not be visible ...'

He swivelled around. There was a glimmer of admiration in his eyes.

'You are an intelligent woman, Roopmati. It is true, on a rainy day, even on a cloudy day, you will not be able to see the Narmada from the pavilion. But that does not mean you will not be able to touch her waters.'

There was a short silence.

'You speak in riddles, *Huzoor*.'

'Sadiya, tomorrow morning, order the palki and take Bibijaan down to the Rewa Kund to bathe.'

'The Rewa Kund?' Roopmati's voice was puzzled.

'That is the pond of water near my palace, close to the pavilion you went up to today. It was once a spring that came right up through the hills from the Narmada and bubbled here. It was built into a large tank by early Hindu rulers, so the waters of the Rewa Kund are really the waters of the holy Narmada. It is always there for you to worship, to bathe in, to sit by the side of, whenever you cannot see the river from up here.'

Roopmati rose up quickly, her palms joined together, and looked up at him.

'*Huzoor*, I cannot express my gratitude to you enough.'

'I do not want your gratitude, Roopmati. I want your music. Promise me, that from tomorrow, we will be artiste and muse, teacher and pupil.'

Her eyes lit up and she shook her head.

'No, *huzoor*, we shall be partners in composing poetry and music, and in singing together. I can think of no singer more accomplished than you to share my art with.'

He took one last long look at her face, then nodded and strode to the door and disappeared into the darkness.

Chapter 10

Roopmati's days began to settle into a pattern. She would rise early, while it was still dark, bathe and then sit by the window to do *riyaz*. The sky would just be turning a lighter shade of indigo playfully tinged with orange and pink and gold. As she played the tanpura and sang, Roopmati would watch with wondering eyes the world lighting up and it was another kind of music to her, an art recreated morning after morning. The birds would chirp and cheep and warble in the branches of the tamarind trees, some trying to match their *sur* to hers while others drowned her song with theirs. Sadiya would be there, padding around, re-arranging the bolsters and cushions, lovingly dusting the instruments arranged along the walls. It was an hour of the day that was so perfect that Roopmati forgot her home far down in the plains for some time. But she never forgot her river; everything she did or thought or dreamt was only an offering to her.

'*Riyaz* over, Bibijaan?' Sadiya's soft voice drifted into her consciousness as she sat still, lost in the silence of peace, her hands still holding the tanpura.

She smiled and turned towards her companion.

'Yes, Sadiya. Now it is time.'

They made their way out of the mahal, Roopmati holding a silver *thaal* with fruits and flowers and a small diya.

The breezes were gentle at this time of the morning up on the roof of the pavilion. Roopmati placed the puja *thaal* on the ground and then stood gazing at the river shimmering like a gold zari thread in the morning sunshine.

How many moods of you do I see, my river! Sparkling with laughter at sunrise ... then when the world lights up, calmly blue as the sky above ... swishing past, carrying the cold mountain waters down to lands where they are thirsting for you! Sometimes a deep dark green, as secret as the forests you skirt. And when the monsoon clouds break over you, you hold out your arms and embrace the muddy swelling waters in them as they thunder past. Oh mother, teach me to be a woman like you, loving and giving and holding all the pain and smiling through.

Roopmati held up a small copper pot with water in which floated some tulsi leaves and offered it to the Narmada, tilting the vessel to spill a few drops at a time as she prayed, held up the plate of fruits to the river and reverently touched its rim to her brow. She threw a few flowers in the direction of the river and concluding the ritual, placed the ghee filled diya on the palm of her hand. Shielding its flickering flame from the breeze, she carefully circled it three times, looking at the river below.

Satisfied at last that she had finished her morning puja, she turned to Sadiya waiting patiently behind her.

'Sadiya, will you accept a fruit from this plate?' she asked hesitantly. 'It's prasad, so if your faith does not permit you to, I understand.'

Sadiya smiled a wise old smile and raised her tiny left hand to take it.

'Your right hand, Sadiya,' Roopmati said with affection in her voice.

They went down the steps in companionable silence.

Roopmati felt content, complete ... and yes, charged, to begin her new life in Mandu.

The evening gathering of music lovers, the *mehfil,* would begin after the day cooled and the sun sank, leaving the world poised and quivering with anticipation, a cacophony of bird calls filling the ears like clamouring silver bells. The evening skies would scurry away to dress themselves up in honour of another bewitching night in Mandu. They would return when the lamps had been lit all over the city and the sounds of music and *ghungroos* rang in the air; and they would glimmer gold in the waters of the lakes and fountains and flicker silver in the shadows of the forests. So enticing was the night life of the city, that they say even the creatures of the day, the peacock and the pigeon and the partridge, would hide behind pillars and in the crevices of rafters to catch a glimpse of the celebrations, night after night, in hall after hall.

In the Shahi Mahal, a knot of women, their faces covered by low-hanging *ghungats,* would gather in the main hall of audience, plush with its carpets and cushions and wide windows overlooking the Munj Talab and the illuminated complex of palaces. The evening would begin with the tuning of their instruments, a tanpura here and a *been sitar* there, a sarangi here and a tabla there. Soon the air throbbed with the beat of the tabla and the drone of the tanpura setting the pitch.

The women musicians would begin to play, building up the tempo, making the very walls and pillars vibrate, creating a suitable setting for the grand entry of the Sultan of Malwa. As he walked in, they would rise as one, bowing low over their palms ... *aadaab, aadaab* ... and move back to sit near the walls. Baz would take his place at the centre, adjusting his *chogha* and pyjama, his hair free and flowing to his shoulders and his beard trimmed and tight around surprisingly vulnerable lips.

He would pick up his *been sitar*, that extension of his very self which transformed his feelings and emotions into melody. As he drew the first notes, the air was rent with cries of *wah, wah, wah*! Completely unaware of his audience as he sank into the composition, Baz would play with his eyes closed, his features set in an expression of rapture. At the end, when he opened his eyes, there would be a thunder of appreciation, followed by an anticipatory hush. A tiny figure would totter into the chamber, salute him low and announce in her deep, dark voice, 'Sultan-e-Malwa, Badshah-e-jahan, I solicit your permission to announce the entry of Bibijaan Roopmati, Ustad-e-mosiqui, the Sultan's personal musician in Mandu, the city of Shadiabad, the precious jewel of Malwa ...'

Baz smiled and raised his hand. Sadiya backed to the door, waving her palm to and from her chin. As Baz watched, Roopmati walked in slowly, her palms joined together in a namaste. She was dressed in a cotton *neevi* of a mustard colour with a border woven in dark brown and pale green thread, her hair loosely plaited down to her hips. A red bindi adorned her forehead, but beyond that, she wore no adornments. As she settled down, her gaze shyly sought the other singers and the audience seated along the walls, and meeting their eyes through zari-worked veils, she smiled gently.

Baz and Roopmati faced each other, and the evening began. As Roopmati's fingers stroked the strings of the tanpura, Baz began with his favourite raga, Bhoopali, and she joined him in perfect unison as they wound their way through the intricacies of the *chalan*s and *pakad*s.

As the night progressed and they moved on to the ragas Tilak Kamod, Jog and Shahana, the audience watched and listened, mesmerised by these two masters of the land.

It was well past the midnight hour when Baz stopped and looking around, bowed his head and raised his fingers to his brow. Immediately, all the women rose and returned his salute as they filed out. Finally, it was only the two of them left. Still mired in the music and the aura of the evening, they sat speechless. Roopmati finally moved the tanpura away and rose.

'It is late, *Huzoor*; I will retire now.'

He nodded. 'That was a beautiful *jugalbandi*. It appears, we were made to sing together.' He rose. 'Until tomorrow then.'

She stood watching him until he walked out of the door. His height and stature, his easy, loose-limbed walk and his gentle, sweet nature were beginning to haunt her days and she could barely wait for the evening when she would see him at last and sing with him. She put a hand to her fast beating heart.

He is the Sultan, I am his singer. There is and never will be anything more between us. He has his begum and his dancing girls and his harem of women to choose from.

'Bibijaan?' Sadiya's voice was lost in the sounds of the pigeons that had started their warbling in the rafters outside the window again.

Roopmati stood at the window and watched the Munj Talab growing darker, listened to the fading sounds of music and laughter and *ghungroos*.

And I have my music and my father's visits to wait for...

She felt the tears welling up in her eyes and watched the lights grow and blur and tremble.

Chapter 11

Roopmati's father never arrived. A month after she came to Mandu, the Sultan sent a palki and two horsemen to bring him back. They returned empty-handed.

'*Huzoor,* Thakur Thaan Singh was unable to accompany us to visit his daughter, because his old mother had just expired, and he has to perform all the rituals for her departed soul.'

When Roopmati heard this, she felt sadness tinged with a kind of relief. Her grandmother, blind and completely unaware of her surroundings, had been a great responsibility for her father. At least he would now be free to come and visit her, perhaps even come to live here with her in this palace. She felt a sudden surge of hope within her. She would speak to the Sultan about it. Yes, she would ask ... no, insist ... that her father sell his cattle, hire out his farmlands to another farmer and move to Mandu to live out the remainder of his years in the company of his daughter.

Her eyes sparkled with joy as she spoke to the Sultan that evening. He stared at her face, his breath catching in his chest at the sheer beauty of her face, specially her eyes, large and limpid and guileless.

'*Huzoor,* I have a request to make of you. Now that my father is free of my grandmother's responsibility, I would like to propose that he move here to live with me in this palace.' There was a few seconds' silence and she hastened to add, 'Or perhaps I should say, I need your permission to have him move here permanently.'

Baz could not believe that it could be so easy to please this maiden. He nodded, trying hard to keep the eagerness out of his voice.

'Roopmati, this is now your home. Your father is more than welcome to come and share it with you. Please send a messenger down to the plains and convey the message to him as an invitation from me.'

In two days' time, the messenger returned to tell her that the Thakur had asked for a few months time to sell his cattle and lands. Roopmati waited impatiently, her thoughts with her father as she imagined him in his humble little home, putting his affairs in order so that he could undertake the journey as soon as possible to be with her.

~

A few days later, all thoughts of her father were sucked out of Roopmati's mind and heart one morning, when she was in the garden of the Shahi Mahal. Walking around the grounds that bordered the Munj Talab, she looked across the waters at the Jahaz Mahal, shaped like a ship anchored between two water bodies.

She knew it to be the zenana, and spent some time looking at its imposing stone facade with ornate balconies overlooking the lake. She tried to imagine the women who lived there, whose days must be spent in beautifying themselves and practising song and dance to perform for the Sultan and his nobles every night. She wondered what they must think and feel and dream of ... did they joke and tease and laugh together, or were they sullen and cynical, hardened by being viewed only as objects of desire, playthings for a night or two? Were they like birds in a cage, yearning to fly free?

She shook her head ruefully.

I too am a bird in a cage, but the difference is that I am caged here for my art and not for my body. And art must be shared and enjoyed with rasikas. But if I were not treated with respect by the Sultan and his servants, I would never stay.

She seated herself on a stone bench below a profusely flowering tabua tree and inspired by the calls of a koel in the boughs, she tried to pen a couplet. She wrote slowly with pointed chalk on stretched, indigo-dyed cloth.

Voice of an angel, showering your favours on me
As the tree showers her petals down
Your song has shrouded all my griefs
And buried them, covered with flowers.

There was a rustle behind her and she started, thinking it was a deer that had wandered in from the forest. But before she could turn, a deep voice made her freeze in her seat.

'I can see that Mandu is adulating your beauty and talent in her own special way.'

He lifted his chin almost imperceptibly. She looked up at the tree from where the golden yellow blossoms were floating down and felt blood rush to her face in embarrassment. Unable to turn and look into Baz's eyes, she continued to sit, staring down at the writing log in her hands.

A large hand came down and picked it up. She waited, lower lip bitten down with shyness. He read the lines out and the deep timbre in his voice set off a strange quiver behind her navel. 'Voice of an angel, hmm, these couplets could well describe my feelings too.'

In the short silence that followed, the koel outdid itself, pouring forth its notes with joyous abandon. Baz replaced the log on the bench and held out a silk wrapped package to her.

Roopmati hesitantly took it and glanced up at him questioningly.

'Open it.'

She unrolled the cloth and a thick, cloth bound notebook fell into her lap. She opened it and reverently rifled through the fine white sheets within, then looked up at him with shining eyes.

'Zafarshani paper from Gujarat,' Baz said. 'Nothing but the best for my poet and composer.' He gave her a partridge quill from his pocket, and added, 'Sadiya will give you more quills and a pot of ink. For obvious reasons, I could not be seen riding around with ink spilling out of the pockets of my *chogha*!'

She gave a gurgle of laughter at the image, then looked up and caught his lopsided grin. They burst into laughter and it was like the moment had blotted out everything else in the universe.

But in seconds, he was gone and she felt a thrust of something akin to longing in her chest. Suddenly, the evening hour seemed too far away and the colours of the garden, a little paler. She held the notebook to her chest all the way back to her chamber.

~

Sadiya was a talker.

Roopmati had realised early in their association that Sadiya could talk continuously, if not interrupted; even distractions did not work for long. She would just pick up the thread and carry on as if she had not been side-tracked at all.

It amused Roopmati, and sometimes it actually entertained her, because she herself was not too communicative by nature. Besides, the chatter was by no means uninteresting. Sadiya was full of information. She would talk about the city of Mandu, its monuments, its lakes, its gateways, its traditions. She could talk intelligently about chess and music and polo and tiger hunting. And she could be argumentative too, ready for a debate on any topic, either for or against! Roopmati would sometimes express her opinion on something and Sadiya would deliberately prove her wrong, just for the fun of it. Being with Sadiya was so mentally stimulating, that for the first time in her life, Roopmati began to enjoy spending time with a peer. As unlike as they were in looks and deportment, they developed a friendship hard to define or name.

There was one thing they had both agreed on, from the beginning. They did not like Panna, the eunuch who stood guard outside the front entrance to the Shahi Mahal. Having been appointed by the Sultan himself, Panna strutted around full of self-importance. But that was not why he was disliked. Roopmati found his stern expression unpleasant and Sadiya whispered that she had once found him listening to their conversation from outside the window.

'Oh Sadiya, he probably only wants to know what we women talk about in our chambers,' Roopmati had pacified her. 'What harm can his listening to our silly chatter do?'

Sadiya made a face and shrugged her shoulders. 'I don't like him.'

'Well, don't let it bother you and don't ever let the Sultan know your feelings. I am obliged to him for all the comforts and protection he has given me and would not like to seem ungrateful.' She loosened her long hair from its braid for Sadiya to brush and plait, knowing how much she loved to do it.

'Come, help me get ready for the evening *mehfil*, pick out a *neevi* for me to wear. How about this one?'

Sadiya shook her head.

'No, Bibijaan, no more *neevi* and *aasana* for you.' At Roopmati's surprised look, she opened the brass studded wooden trunk and took out an armful of fabrics in earth hues from it and arranged them on the bed, then carefully placed an embroidered, gem encrusted choli next to each.

Roopmati gasped. The combinations were stunning.

'What is this, Sadiya?' she asked, her hand still at her mouth.

'They are sarees I ordered for you. Woven from the finest cotton in Malwa. And thread-worked cholis made by our own tailors here, who have learned the art from the Mughals of Agra. You will now wear only these beautiful pieces at your *mehfils* with the Sultan. No more coarse cotton *neevis* and thickly woven *asanas* for you, Bibijaan.'

'But ... but why?'

'Because music such as yours deserves the best, Bibijaan.'

Roopmati unrolled a soft cotton length in deep green and holding it to her cheek, looked teasingly at Sadiya, knowing what her little companion would say.

Sadiya struck her brow dramatically.

'Oh, Bibijaan, you choose always green! I know that it makes your skin look creamy and, of course, your kohl-lined eyes match this black border, but I think the Sultan would like to see you in other colours too!'

Roopmati coloured in confusion.

'I ... I don't dress for him, Sadiya! How did you think ... why, that is a ridiculous idea! He comes there to hear me sing. What I wear doesn't matter. Here, you decide what colour I should wear today.'

'This same colour that you wore only yesterday?' Sadiya held up a cream coloured *neevi* mischievously and winked.

Roopmati's eyes widened and she started to protest, then closed her lips tight. She nodded.

'Of course. Anything.' She watched in relief as Sadiya laid out the green sari and matched it with fine-cut jade jewellery.

In her mind she could see the Sultan's eyes as they fell on her every evening. It bothered her that the look in them had become more important to her than his eyes closed in rapture as she sang.

Chapter 12

Jana Begum had a lot on her mind, and when she was deeply preoccupied thus, she would order the maidservant to leave her alone and sit by the window of her small and spartan chamber for hours. But today, she sat there and waited for her visitor with impatience. There was so little time and so much to do.

Finally, there was a soft cough at the half-open door and a messenger drifted in.

She looked at him sharply.

'Well, you have taken your time! Eleven days to bring me news of my nephew from Delhi?'

'Begum Sahiba, I regret that there has been a delay in bringing you reports of Adham Khan Sahib, esteemed *sipahisalar* of Jahanpanah Akbar. But he was on a campaign, south of Agra, and I waited to hear of his return so that I may convey the same to you.'

'Well? When does he return to Akbar's court?'

'Any day now. There has been great success in his capture of the Gwalior Fort, and he is expected to return triumphant to great accolades and rewards from the Emperor himself.'

'Good!' For the first time, Jana Begum's face softened in a half smile. She was fond of her half-sister's son. 'I am glad to hear of his victories. This means that the time has come for him to wine and dine and partake of the pleasures of the court. And so, what better time for me to send this message? Write it down!'

She pointed to a roll of parchment paper lying on the table. The man hastily picked it up, clipped it to a board and sat on the ground, quill and ink at hand and looked up at her expectantly.

Jana Begum rose and began to pace the floor as she dictated.

'My dear nephew, It has been many moons since I heard from you, but I always hear *of* you and your eminent status in the Jahanpanah's court as the man who single-handedly leads the Emperor's armies to battle and conquers over new territories for his crown. Felicitations to you, dear Adham, on your latest victories in Gwalior. I am, as always, very proud to call you my own.'

'Well, it is time now to sit back and taste the fruits of your success, namely the sparkling amusements of the court, the dance and music, songs and shows. To that end, I send you news of a new voice that Emperor Akbar will surely want to add to his *khazana* of *anmol ratans*. This is a woman called Roopmati, who was discovered singing on the banks of the Narmada river by my son-in-law, Baz Bahadur. She is a classical singer so talented and so accomplished in her art that she can only enthral the Emperor—that connoisseur of every virtuosity—and thereby, bring fame upon you as the man who brought her into his court. Can anyone dare to flout or even question an order from the Emperor, even if it is camouflaged as a request? I think not indeed! Awaiting your response I remain, ever, your affectionate Khalajaan.'

She waited for the man to leave and then opened her *paan daan* with a small smile on her lips.

Never play a game without pawns. I have made my move, now to wait for the king to send his men and claim the queen from the other side. Oh my foolish daughter, what would you ever do without your Ammi *by your side?*

Hiba sucked the finger tips of her left hand and then looked at them again. They were raw and painful. Learning to play the sarangi was so difficult, she was tempted to give up yet again. Ever since Baz had devoted his life to the pleasures of music, she had been advised by her mother to take up an instrument so that she may be able to hold his interest, at least some of the time.

'You cannot sing nor even pick up a note correctly to save your life, my dear child,' Jana Begum had informed her drily. 'But perhaps you may be able to just ... er ... pluck the strings of an instrument when he is within earshot; all we need is to let him think that you are interested in what he is so passionate about.'

Hiba had called in a teacher and tried several times to get the hang of it; left finger tips curved around the neck of the sarangi, bow in right hand. Press a string, pull the bow, press two strings, pull, now press only second string ...

'Aah! It is cutting my skin!' she would cry and pushing the instrument away, dismiss the teacher.

But now that she knew that it was a matter of keeping Baz in her life or losing him to that woman forever, she gritted her teeth and began to follow what the teacher was doing.

I will learn to play for Baz if it kills me. Even now these strings are killing me with pain.

~

As Roopmati tuned the strings of the sarangi, her eyes constantly turned to the door at the far end of the hall, unconsciously willing a tall silhouette to fill its emptiness. Although the Sultan only came here in the evenings for the *mehfil* she had started expecting him to turn up anywhere, at any time, after that encounter in the garden. There had been something magical about that afternoon. The low hanging clouds sending messages on cool breezes of the coming rains, the calling birds, the flowering, showering trees, the grass springy under her bare feet. And then, his deep voice behind her. Even now, when she thought of that moment, she felt a shiver in the back of her neck. But it disturbed her; these thoughts, these tingling sensations, and this constant sense of anticipation as if she was waiting for something, someone.

She turned her thoughts to her father. May be her restlessness was because of her anxiety about him. How was he? When would he be ready to come here to live with her? Supposing he changed his mind and decided to stay on in his little house? How sad and disappointed she would be!

She confided her thoughts to Sadiya that afternoon.

'I am afraid that my father may never come here to live with me. He is a proud man, Sadiya, and would prefer to be in his own house, rather than live as a permanent guest of the Sultan.'

Sadiya considered this for a few moments and then spoke in her deep, honey voice.

'Bibijaan, the Thakur may be a proud man, but not too proud I am sure, to throw away this chance to see you every day. My suggestion is, when he comes, ask the Sultan to give him some work to keep him occupied. May be he could manage our farms here. We do grow all our fruits and vegetables and some grains and keep livestock for meat, you know!'

'What a wonderful idea, Sadiya! Yes, when *Baba* arrives, I will indeed insist that he be kept employed in some work.' She looked at the sky.

'I would like to take a walk near the forested area in the south, Sadiya. The rain clouds have not yet built up.'

'If Bibijaan rides, I could ask for a horse for you. That way, you can return quickly before a thunderstorm sets in.'

'Hmm ... yes, I do ride, but will the Sultan be alright with my taking one of his horses?'

'Oh Bibijaan! The Sultan has only one complaint against you! That you do not use any of the conveniences he has made available to you for day and night! Your big palki, the gentle mare Ruksana, your retinue of servants that you never call for, the silks and jewels that you refuse to wear except at the *mehfil*!'

'I am a simple village girl, Sadiya. I don't even know what to do with all this luxury!' She hesitated, then said shyly, 'Yes, I would like to take Ruksana for a ride today.'

'I will send Panna with you, Bibijaan; you cannot go alone.'

'Oh no no Sadiya, I would like to ride alone with my thoughts. I promise to be back soon.'

Sadiya bowed albeit reluctantly and backed away. Roopmati continued sitting dreamily in the garden. What had she ever done to deserve all this beauty? Suddenly she felt a thrust of guilt. Had she forgotten her river so soon? Beyond getting a glimpse of the distant waters every morning, there was little homage she had paid to her since coming to Mandu.

Caught in the whirlpool of this enchanting land, can I forget the swirling eddies that shaped me ... my river, my mother, my muse, and the source of all my melody?

She mounted the mare and sat sideways, arranging the folds of her *neevi* carefully across both knees on the left flank of the horse, then held the reins closely as the animal cantered down the path. There was poetry in their bodies moving as one; there was a deep understanding, one woman to another. Roopmati laughed in sheer exhilaration.

'Ruksana ... you are beautiful, do you know that?' The mare's ears twitched backwards in reply.

Coming to a point where the path headed straight to the south western gate, where she had entered Mandu not so long ago, and branched left towards the Sultan's palace and the pavilion, from which she viewed the river every day, Roopmati hesitated.

Today she would do penance for loving this city so much that she had forgotten how the Narmada felt to the touch. Today she would stand in her holy waters and meditate on her river.

She turned the mare's head and started down the path leading to the Sultan's palace and next to it, the Rewa Kund.

Roopmati stood knee deep in the Rewa Kund and bent to scoop from the still, clear depths of the pond. She sprinkled some water on her head and touched her palms to her face.

'Ma Narmada, bless me,' she said as she carried the water to her lips. 'Ma Narmada, bless the song on my tongue that it may never dry up. And Ma Narmada. bless this beautiful city and these good people that they may thrive and prosper!'

There was a slight sound behind her, like the scrunch of dry leaves underfoot. She turned and saw the Sultan standing under a tree, near Ruksana, holding the reins of his own horse.

Suddenly conscious of the folds of her garment clinging wetly to her legs, she turned back, hoping he would go away. But Baz laughed and said, 'My horse recognised Ruksana, Roopmati, not my fault!' There was a deep roll of thunder and the sky darkened perceptibly. 'You had better hurry if you don't want to go from half wet to fully wet!'

Roopmati looked up and the first big drops fell on her face. She hastily stepped out of the water and came up the sloping bank. Lightning cracked open the skies, thunder crashed and the rain came down in sheets, drenching them both to the skin.

Baz threw his shawl over her shoulders and holding the reins of both horses, led the way towards his palace on the other bank of the kund.

'Come as fast as you can! We should not be standing under the trees in this storm!'

She walked with difficulty, her wet clothes catching her legs. But there was no way out; she had to take shelter in Baz's palace until the storm passed.

Chapter 13

The Baz Bahadur Mahal was so stately and graceful that it would have taken her breath away, if she had not been screwing her eyes up against the stinging onslaught of raindrops. She stumbled on the wide and shallow stone stairway rising gently to the arched passage of the entrance and he put out a hand to steady her and let it remain on her arm, as if it were the most natural thing in the world. Secretly grateful for the support, Roopmati followed Baz down the passage, past a small courtyard and through another passage that turned, taking them away from any prying eyes. Finally, they came through a wide opening beyond which she could make out a second, larger courtyard barely visible in the rain. But instead of coming out into it, Baz turned into a doorway on the left. They entered a hall graced with such high ceilings and tall windows that even in the darkened afternoon, it seemed full of light and air.

Roopmati stood dignified in her dripping clothes and looked up and all around admiringly.

'This is my private audience hall,' he said softly and it dawned on her that he was not just an attractive young man and a singer, but a king in his palace and ruler of all he surveyed.

'I will ask my man to bring you a set of fresh clothes and you can change and partake of refreshments with me,' he continued. 'You know, I too need an opportunity to offer you hospitality in my home.'

Her eyes flew up, and lips opened, ready to retort that the whole of Mandu was his domain, and she was but his guest wherever she wandered. Then she caught his teasing look and stopped. He gave a short bark of laughter.

'You are too serious, Roopmati. Come, let us sit together and have some wine and get to know each other more than merely as singers.'

She shook her head firmly.

'Thank you, *Huzoor,* but I have to refuse your kind offer. I will be on my way as soon as the rain reduces a little. Sadiya will be anxiously waiting for me.'

He nodded and pointed to a seat.

'Sadiya will be informed, don't worry.' She sat down, still holding the shawl around her.

Baz sat down on a low cane *moda* in front of her, folding his long legs with difficulty, and for the first time, they looked at each other as man and woman, without the ethereal magic of music turning the air hazy around them. Overhead, in the wooden beams, the rumbling of the pigeons grew louder as the sounds of rain outside became softer.

'Roopmati,' Baz said, a little huskily, then cleared his throat. 'There is something I have been meaning to say to you, ever since I brought you here to Mandu.'

Her eyes darted to the window as if seeking an escape. Heart thudding, she started to rise.

'No, no, please don't get worried. I just wanted to tell you a little about myself.'

She sank down again, almost holding her breath. There was so much she wanted to know about him, but had been too shy to ask anyone, in case it was misunderstood as shameless interest in an attractive man. Besides, he was a powerful ruler and her enquiries might have led to gossip that she was craving his favours.

'I am married, Roopmati,' he said, looking into her eyes. 'Yes, I have a Sultana who I was married to many years back, when I was too young to know what I wanted. She lives here, in Mandu. But I have no relationship with her.' He shook his head and shrugged his broad shoulders. 'Of course, when I was younger, there was the hot blood of youth and we shared a bed and many moments, but ...'

Roopmati felt a strange twisting in her stomach.

'Why are you telling me all this?' she asked frowning inwardly, but trying to sound calm. 'Surely your private life does not concern me.'

He lifted a hand. 'Wait, Roopmati, I have not finished what I wanted to tell you. Well, Hiba—that is her name—and I have moved apart over the years and while I honour her position as the Sultana, there is little I feel for her. I have not visited her palace for years, except to wish her on the occasions of Id.' He rubbed his jaw thoughtfully. 'If you ask me why, I don't know really. All I can say is that we don't share any interests. I have my music and my poetry and my hunting and fencing and she doesn't enjoy any of those.' He paused and gazed at the intricately carved wooden pillar on the opposite side of the room. Then he nodded and turned to Roopmati with a lopsided smile, making her breath catch again.

'Confession over. Your turn.'

'What?' She blinked in consternation.

His laugh was infectious, making her lips twitch in response. Then he sobered up and continued, looking into her eyes.

'Roopmati, your life is an open book, very clean and unmarked and untouched. I cannot claim to have led a life like that. I have had a turbulent youth, with its share of drinking and smoking opium and frolicking with women. There have been brawls and bloodshed. But after meeting you, that is all in the past. All I want to do is be worthy of you, your singing.'

She bit her lower lip and gazed at him in wonder.

Worthy of me or worthy of my singing? Which of them does he mean?

Baz continued. 'Roopmati, I want to say this just once and I will never say it again. You have cast some kind of a spell over me and I would like nothing better than to make you my wife.' His words were drowned by the agitated sounds of the pigeons in the rafters and she wondered if she had heard them right at all.

'When I first saw you, I wanted to bring you here as my court singer. And then, something happened, and I found I could not share you with everyone. So when I brought you here, it was on the condition to you, and to your father, that you would be my personal musician and singing partner. Then ...' He raised his hands in simple surrender, 'I saw how dedicated you were to your art, how pure of purpose, and I made a promise to myself that first evening that I would never, ever consider you anything other than my goddess of music, my singing partner ...'

Roopmati looked at him, deeply touched by his confession, and yet, faintly, very slightly disappointed in some place of her heart that was still unexplored. She opened her mouth to say something, but nothing came out and she closed it again.

'No, no, you need not answer that. I just wanted to express my feelings, but as I have told you before, I am a man of my word and will never force you into something you do not want.' He looked out of the window. 'The rain has stopped, you can leave now.' His cheeks creased in sudden mirth as he contemplated her form huddled in the shawl.

'Seeing you clinging to my shawl like that for life, I doubt that you will return it to me until you get home and change your wet clothes.'

As they walked back to the entrance, she realised that her clothes were not wet any more. Her body was burning with a strange heat and she longed to get back to her chamber and throw off the shawl. As she mounted from a stone culvert and turned the horse's head, he saluted her formally. '*Allah hafiz.*'

The path that she had come down, enjoying the beauty of the meadows around her, was a blur to her all the way back. Another sudden shower didn't help.

She was greeted by Sadiya at the entrance of Shahi Mahal. A stable boy helped her dismount and led Ruksana away. Sadiya chattered as they went into her chambers.

'Oh Bibijaan, I became so anxious as the first drops began to fall! Here on the plateau, thunder and lightning in the monsoons can be very dangerous you know. I did not know if you were under a tree, you know. The *tailapatra* tree, maybe because of its tall trunk and skinny branches, seems to attract lightning but luckily, most people don't stand under it because it doesn't offer much shelter from the rain, you know!' She looked up at Roopmati with a laugh, then narrowed her eyes and fell silent.

Roopmati allowed Sadiya to peel off her wet clothes and sat on a stool wrapped in a towel as she vigorously dried her long hair. The little woman finally spoke.

'Bibijaan, did we meet anyone?' She sometimes added herself to her mistress's activities, bizarre though it sounded.

Roopmati mumbled through the thick fabric covering her head.

'Hmm.' Sadiya said, 'I thought as much.'

'What?' Roopmati parted the towel and peeped out of its folds. 'What did you say?'

'What did *you* say?'

'Nothing.'

'*Theek hai.* I thought you said we met the Sultan. I must be mistaken.'

The towelling completed, Sadiya went to take out fresh clothes from the trunk. Roopmati ran her fingers through her tangled hair, her hands still unsteady and her breath far from calm. Then on a sudden whim, she put out a hand.

'Sadiya, wait ... give me one of my old clothes to wear. I will not be attending the *mehfil* tonight.'

Sadiya turned slowly, hugging the beautifully worked peacock blue sari and bright pink blouse she had chosen and gazed at Roopmati full of concern.

'Oh Bibijan, are we ill? I am so sorry, I did not think that getting caught in the rain may cause you to fall sick! You wear dry clothes and lie down, I will go and boil you some ginger chai and bring you *dhoop* pieces thrown into a pan of burning coals to place near your damp hair!'

'No, no, Sadiya, I am not ...' Her words petered off lamely as Sadiya hurried away. She groaned and buried her face in her hands. Her mind was churning with confused thoughts, her heart thudding with conflicting emotions.

Did the Sultan actually say what he did? Did he say he wanted to make me his wife? No, no, it cannot be ... I must have misheard. He must have said something else ... he spoke softly and the pigeons, curse them, were so noisy! And ... and then to add to all my confusion, he said that he would only say it once and never say it again! How will I ever know?

Roopmati sat hugging herself with her arms around her body, suddenly feeling cold and vulnerable. Sadiya returned with a large silver tray on which sat a jug of steaming chai, a plate of *kachoris* and an iron *karhai* of burning coals. She busied herself setting it all up, giving a running commentary of how she proposed to take care of her mistress, how she would send word to the Sultan about the evening gathering and how Panna was a useless chowkidar because he was nowhere around when Bibijaan was to be greeted at the gate and helped off the horse and when coals had to be fanned and piled into an iron pan for Bibijaan's use.

That night, lying in the dark, listening to the distant sounds of music and laughter from Jahaz Mahal across the lake, Roopmati allowed herself to relive the moments in the Sultan's palace.

You have cast some spell over me and I would like nothing better than to make you my wife.

My wife.

She sat up and drew her knees to her chest. Resting her chin on them, she smiled a wan smile. Her heartbeat was high, her face felt warm and her mind confused.

But Sultans don't marry for anything but alliances or heirs ... they drift from one desirable woman to another, taking them to bed but never to heart. I must have heard him wrong. But if he did say it ... well, let me make this very clear ... I am not available ... I can never ever marry him or anyone for that matter! Music is my husband and the river my god. There is no place in my heart or life for any other.

Satisfied with the finality of her thoughts, she lay down and drifted into a fitful sleep where Baz pulled out her sarangi from the waters of the Rewa Kund, wiped it with his shawl and handed it to her.

'Panna threw it in,' he said. The rain began to pour again and as she struggled to play, it was her father in front of her. He shook his head at her and said sadly, 'Your mother died, my child, play a sad song ...'

Chapter 14

It was two weeks since Thakur Thaan Singh had sent word that he would come to live in Mandu once he had sold his farm and settled his affairs. But Roopmati had not noticed, because there was so much else on her mind. In fact, to her chagrin, it was as if there was nothing else but the Sultan. Wherever she looked, she saw his face, his light brown eyes, the high bridged nose and tender lips that belied the arrogance of power and wealth she had always believed he had. But now she knew. She knew Baz Bahadur was a man of warmth and sensitivity, and most important, a man of his word.

Roopmati had come to dread the meetings with the Sultan, sitting across from him, evening after evening as they sang together. The day she had come back from his palace, drenched and befuddled, Sadiya had sent word to him that her mistress was unwell. It gave Roomati a chance to avoid the *mehfil* for a few days. Moreover, Roopmati was relieved to learn that Baz would soon leave on a hunting expedition that was likely to keep him away for about ten days.

Sadiya had brought her the news early one morning when she came with hot water in a heavy and ornate silver jug for Roomati's morning drink. She talked as she poured the water, squeezed half a lemon into it and stirred in a spoonful of honey.

'Ten days, Bibijaan, ten days he will be away! And we have not sung with him for the last three days now, what with your sore throat since that day in the rain!' Roopmati squirmed. There was no sore throat. She hated to lie, but what could she have said to Sadiya ...

I cannot face the Sultan because suddenly our relationship has shifted from singing partners to man and woman? I feel strange and shy now. I cannot meet his eyes without thinking of what he said.

For the next few days, Roopmati moped around listlessly, in the garden, in her bedroom, on the terrace. Hopefully Sadiya would not be astute enough to guess the real reason.

She held the thick notepad full of smooth white sheets in her hands, buried her face in it and inhaled deeply. There was a faint smell of musk on the sheets. Was it from the Sultan's hands, the scent of his very masculine perfume? Lost in thought, Roopmati did not pen a single word on them. She reasoned with herself, scolded herself, even tried to shame herself out of these thoughts, but there was no change in the feverish state of her body and mind.

Roopmati, you are a singer, an artiste, disciple of one of the most revered gurus in all of Malwa, you cannot get swayed by the Sultan's easy words and looks! Why, he must be speaking like this to every young woman he meets! Yes, that's it ... he tried to proposition me to see if I would fall into his arms like all those other women. He does not know that I am not interested in romance and relationships. I live only for my music.

Partly satisfied with her conclusions, she took a deep breath and began to walk back from the garden towards the Shahi Mahal, when she sighted Sadiya hurrying towards her, her face agitated and her tiny *sharara* pants flapping against her legs.

'Bibijaan, Bibijaan!' she cried out from a distance, 'There is a messenger who has come for you!'

Roopmati frowned, puzzled. She could only think of her father. Had he sent word that he was ready to move to Mandu? It was most unlike him. She had expected that she would have to send several messages to him before he would agree to actually come here.

As Roopmati and Sadiya hurried to the house, they found a farmer from her village waiting at the door, Panna standing guard beside him. The man was dressed in the traditional white dhoti and kurta, with a white turban on his head. Roopmati folded her hands in a namaste, studying his weathered, sunburnt face. His eyes looked sad and resigned.

'What is it, Bhaisaheb?' She asked him gently. 'I hope everything is well at home?'

He shook his head and the furrows on his face deepened as he replied, 'No, behen, the news is not good. Your father passed away two days back. He was found in the field by my dog, who stood by the body, barking away until I reached there.'

Roopmati felt the faces sway around her. She put out a hand to hold on to something. Sadiya quickly came to her side and shouted to Panna to help get Bibijaan into the house. The next few minutes were a blur for Roopmati. When she opened her eyes, she found herself on the carpet of the main hall, supported by cushions. She fought a wave of nausea as the farmer narrated his story. 'Your father must have been out in the rain, driving his cows into their shed when he must have collapsed. We think it was chest pain, because his hand was still clutching the fabric of his kurta when he was found.'

Roopmati felt a deep, groaning cry emanate from her throat. She doubled up with an almost physical pain and curled up on the floor sobbing. She did not hear the man talking on, until he was interrupted by Sadiya and sent away with Panna to the kitchen to have some food and water.

Sadiya sat down beside her mistress and stroked her head with her little hands, making soothing sounds in her throat.

It was only later—it may have been minutes or several hours that Roopmati became aware of her surroundings. She was on her bed and a maidservant was keeping vigil from her place on the floor. Raising her head that felt like a bale of cotton soaked in water, Roopmati propped herself on an elbow and asked the woman hoarsely, 'Where is Sadiya?' The maid jumped up and muttering that sounded like 'I will call her,' ran out, seeming relieved to hand over charge of her grieving mistress to one so capable.

'Bibijaan?' The honey voice at her side was comforting, causing Roopmati to break down again. 'Sadiya ... my ... my father ... I was waiting to see him! I wanted to spend the rest of my days taking care of him!' She hiccoughed. 'He has done so much for me. I never had a chance to do *seva* for him ...'

'Yes, yes, Bibijaan,' crooned Sadiya, 'I know, I understand ...' She sat on the bed and held Roopmati's hand.

'Sadiya, where is my bhai from the village? Has he eaten something? He has travelled a long way to give me this news.'

'Do not worry yourself, Bibijaan. We have made sure he ate well, and he was taken to the caravansarai to rest awhile. His horse was stabled and fed too.'

Roopmati sank back on her pillow in relief, then sat up again as her mind cleared.

'Sadiya ... have they done my father's ...' She stopped, her eyes welling up again.

'Yes, they have. They called for your uncle's son to perform the rites. Now his *asthi* has been kept in a clay pot for immersion in the river, so ...'

Roopmati closed her eyes and clutched her hands together tightly.

'Thank God! There is still something of him left! I will do the immersion myself, Sadiya! I will flow his ashes in the waters myself. I am going down to the plains today.'

Sadiya hastily got off the bed and shook her great head. 'Please, please, Bibijaan, listen to me. I have sent word to the Sultan. He is barely half a day's ride away and we know in which direction they have gone to hunt. If he starts back as soon as he gets the message, he will be here by nightfall. He will decide how to send you down and with whom. Please, Bibijaan,' now it was Sadiya's turn to fold her hands, 'The Sultan left you in my care and I cannot let you go out of Mandu without his permission.'

Roopmati scrambled off the bed, her face clouding with anger.

'I don't need anybody's permission to leave this city! I am not his slave, nor he my master! Now, Sadiya, please help me prepare to leave immediately.'

Sadiya did not flinch.

'I am sorry, Bibijaan, but I cannot do anything without the Sultan's orders.'

Roopmati stood straight and proud in her crumpled sari and gazed calmly at Sadiya through her swollen eyes.

'I understand. But *I* do not have to wait for his orders, you know. Can you call Panna?' She stopped and added, 'Oh, yes, you need the Sultan's orders to do that, don't you?'

Sadiya watched her mistress walk out of the room, then sank to her knees in despair, knowing Bibijaan would only be subject to more pain when she realised what had ensued in the past hour.

Roopmati walked out of the front door and called out to Panna. He came up the steps slowly, his dark eyes suspicious.

'Panna! Can you please ask my village brother to come here in half an hour? I will be going down to my home with him. Also, ask the stable boy to get Ruksana ready for me.'

Panna scowled.

'It is not possible, Bibijaan. Your brother has already been sent back.'

'Sent back! Without asking me! Who sent him?'

A sly smile flitted over his dour face.

'It was your companion, Sadiya. She asked him to return immediately.'

Roopmati felt a twist of such powerful anger within her chest that her breath was snatched away for a moment. She turned and saw Sadiya at the doorway. Ignoring her, she brushed past, trying to control her trembling limbs.

'Bibijaan! Bibijaan! Please hear me out.' Sadiya hurried after her. She was panting with the effort. 'Bibijaan, I know for sure that the Sultan will be here by nightfall and he will decide what is best for you. I sent your messenger away because the sooner he left, the safer for him. The path back to his village is fraught with dangers from wild animals after dark.'

He could have waited until the morning! We could have gone down together.

'And, Bibijaan, he mentioned that there is no one to milk the cows in the evening as his wife is ill and his son has gone to the neighbouring town to buy medicines and implements for the farm so I thought ...'

Her voice trailed off.

Roopmati saw sense, but refused to relent. She went into her bedroom and sat down next to the open window, allowing the cool breeze to fan her face.

Sadiya sat down on the floor near the door. They remained like that, one lost in her grief and the other watching her wordlessly.

Evening fell, casting its dusky shadows around the room, then night seeped in, melting the greys into an inky darkness. And then, as the lights came on all over Mandu, the flickering flames from sconces and lamps tiptoed in through the window and began to dance on the walls of the room, on the mirrors and on their faces.

The night began to wane, and yet neither of them moved or spoke. It was as if they had made a pact of silence, to see who would last longer. Suddenly, there was the thud of boots on the thickly carpeted floor of the audience hall. The door was pushed open and a tall, broad shouldered silhouette filled the dim opening.

'Roopmati?'

She started at the voice and form that had been haunting her since the last two days.

Sadiya scrambled to her feet and edged out of the room. Baz clapped his hands and barked a peremptory order to Panna behind him.

'The lamps! Light them! Do you not know your duty?'

He waited while the lamps were lit and the hijra left the room. Then he looked at Roopmati, studying her face with concern.

'I am sorry. So very sorry, to hear about your father! I came as soon as I got the message.'

Roopmati lifted her chin and glared at him.

'There was no need for you to come back, *Huzoor*! It is my father who has ... has died ... and it is I who needs to hurry to him. But ...' Her nostrils flared, 'Apparently here in your city, the one who has been bereaved is not allowed to leave. She has to be given permission first!'

Baz pursed his lips thoughtfully and his eyes flickered over her face. They lingered on her blazing eyes and flushed cheeks.

'Hmmm, I can see why you are angry. You have mistaken Sadiya's concern for restriction.'

'Concern! Concern?' By now Roopmati was so angry, her voice had risen and her face had an angry flush. 'She sent away my kinsman without asking me. I wanted to go back to my home with him, but no! I had to await your orders! Do you know what it is like to want to do something desperately and be shackled so that you cannot even move?'

Baz threw up his hands in surrender and gazed at her face in contrition.

'Yes, Roopmati, I do understand. True, my instructions were to Sadiya never to let you go out of Mandu without my permission. But do you know why I did that? Only because I did not want any harm to come to you. You have led a sheltered life and do not know anything about the world outside. That is why I personally escorted you to Mandu some months back. And now,' he paused and came two steps closer. 'I will personally escort you to your home. As soon as day breaks, we shall set out on horseback.'

Roopmati's breathing continued to be ragged, but as his words sank in, her expression slowly softened.

'You ... you will do that? You will come down to the plains with me?'

He bent his head. 'I absolutely will. You have my word that I shall take you to your home where your father's *asthi* awaits immersion in the river. And I shall accompany you back after you complete your duty.'

She nodded slowly.

'And you are a man of your word.' It was a statement, not a question.

Laughter flickered in his eyes or it could have been the lights from the window.

'Thank you. Now, may I suggest that you get some sleep so that we can leave on our journey as soon as the sun rises? The paths are unsafe in the dark.'

She nodded again.

'Yes, Sadiya told me the same thing.' Then she remembered her anger against Sadiya and tightened her lips.

'Sleep well, Roopmati. We shall journey together tomorrow.'

After he left, she lay down on the bed and closing her eyes, tried to think of her father's beloved face. But strangely, it was light brown eyes, warm and tender, that swam before her. The expression in them made her insides go hot and molten.

She slept at last and dreamt of singing by the Narmada with a man seated opposite. He was silent, but she knew that he was there, watching her, waiting for her to come awake.

Chapter 15

'At last!' Jana Begum looked towards the door where the messenger had been ushered in. Her daughter Hiba put up a hand to stop the maid who had been massaging oil into her hair and sat up against the bolsters on the diwan. The maid quietly left the room.

The man bowed deeply and waited for permission to speak.

'Well! You have taken your time returning from Agra! What news from Shahenshah Akbar's court? What did my nephew Adham Khan say in response to my message?'

'Begum Saheba, I rode with barely two stops to Agra to meet Adham Khan, your esteemed nephew, and conveyed your message to him personally. He showed a lot of interest in your suggestion that the Sultan Baz Bahadur's personal musician be sent to the Mughal court as a court singer. He asked me several questions, for which you had fortunately well-equipped me with answers. Then he asked me to wait until he had a personal audience with the emperor, who is also his milk brother, so that he may make this proposal to him.' He paused.

'Well?' Jana Begum and her daughter were hanging on to his every word.

'It was only two days ago that Adham Khan Saheb had the opportunity to speak to the Shahenshah in his private chamber. Soon after, he sent for me and said that the emperor would be greatly interested in adding this jewel to his court.'

Jana Begum's eyes gleamed. She ignored her daughter's gasp and glance towards her, and spoke slowly.

'So has he sent a message for the Sultan by your hands?'

The man shook his head.

'No, Begum Saheba, he did not, because he said that Shahenshah Akbar wishes to send a royal messenger from his court directly to Sultan Bayazid. He said that it would be circumspect and honourable if he made the request through his own channels.'

He bowed his head and awaited further orders.

Jana Begum wrinkled her nose in a gesture of disdain and distaste.

'Go! You have only done half my job!' She turned her back and waited until the door had closed behind the man.

'*Ammijaan*!' Hiba looked at her mother with suppressed excitement. 'It appears that your plan is working! So Roopmati may be sent to Agra?'

There was a soft knock at the door and it opened slowly. Panna slid in, moving his strapping body coyly. He stood before Jana Begum and swayed, playing with the tassels of his sari *pallu* while he waited to be told to speak.

'What news do you bring me today, Panna?''

Panna rolled his eyes dramatically and spoke in a mincing whisper.

'O Begumjaan! What can I say? The news is not good!'

Jana Begum frowned at him sternly.

'That's enough *nautanki*, Panna. Come to the point!'

Panna put his hand on his heart and looked at Jana Begum with a hurt expression.

'You wound me! Has Panna not been there for you whenever you or Sultana Begum needed anything done? Have I ever let you down?'

Jana Begum closed her eyes fighting rising irritation then looked at him with feigned patience.

'Panna.'

'Yes, yes, Begumjaan, I will tell you of today's developments! Today, early morning, as the sun rose, the Sultan left the city with Roopmati!'

'The Sultan! But he had gone on a hunting expedition yesterday, had he not?'

"Yes, he had! But soon after that, Roopmati got news of her father's death in the plains, so he was summoned back and has now accompanied her to her home by the river ... '

Jana Begum pursed her lips in a fit of anger and almost spat like a disdainful camel; she looked around for a spittoon, then changed her mind and narrowed her eyes at Panna.

'Is that the power she has over him? Wah! Then she is more wily than I believed!' She thought for a minute, chewing on the paan, while Hiba played worriedly with her oily tresses and Panna tinkled the glass bangles on his hairy, green-tatooed arms.

Finally, Jana Begum seemed to have come to a decision. Nodding her head, she addressed Panna.

'You have two tasks before you, Panna. First, you will go to the court portrait painter and ask him to meet me here in half an hour. Second, when Roopmati returns, tell her that the Sultana, Hiba Rahima, would like to meet her to pay a condolence visit. Come back and tell me what she says. Understand? Go now.'

Panna giggled and adjusted his sari over the stiff pyramids on his chest.

'Begum Saheba ... these old rags I wear ... '

Jana took out a plain leather pouch from the folds of her garment and extracted some coins from it. Throwing them at Panna, she repeated, 'Go now.'

As the door closed behind the eunuch, she walked to the spittoon, directed a red stream into it, and turned back to Hiba.

'Be ready to fight for your right, my daughter. And wipe that stupid, scared expression from your face. I notice that it is fast becoming a permanent part of you!'

From the time they had left the gates of Mandu, they had not exchanged a single word. He rode ahead and she followed on Ruksana, the sun in their eyes as they came out of Tarapur Gate and the road wound eastwards before starting its descent.

Watching the Nimar valley from different angles, Roopmati remained immersed in her thoughts. Her heart was heavy with sadness, and yet, there was a certain lift she felt whenever she looked at the back of the Sultan's head.

He cares so much for me that he has rushed back only to accompany me! He could have sent a guard with me but no, he wanted to be with me himself in my hour of grief...

Suddenly, he turned around as though he had heard her thoughts and looked into her face enquiringly, and she shook her head with a small smile, as if he had asked a question and she had answered.

They cantered through the dense jungle of the river valley, its birdsong and wildflowers achingly familiar to her. Finally, on the river's bank, they turned their horses and headed towards the grazing lands of her father's farm. As the thatch roofed house came into view, small and squat, the sobs began to bubble up in Roopmati's chest. She had left her grandmother and father barely six months ago, and now both were gone. There was only an empty house to greet her.

Baz dismounted and held her horse while she got down. They walked towards the open door and he waved her in first. Inside, it was dim and cool and smelt of sandalwood incense. In the centre of the room, on the stone floor, sat a clay pot, tied at the mouth with a piece of cloth. Next to it, glowed a small earthen lamp and incense sticks.

Roopmati sank to the floor, racked by sobs. Immediately, a large, plump woman emerged from the inner room.

'Roopmati *beta*, you have come! I am so glad! We were wondering if we should wait for you or flow the *asthi* in the river ourselves.'

Roopmati hugged her aunt and cried until there were no more tears left. Later as they sat holding brass tumblers of hot chai in folded towels, Roopmati's aunt told her of Thaan Singh's last weeks.

'After his *Amma* died, he was not himself at all. You had left,' she shot an apologetic glance at Baz, 'and he may have felt that there was no one else in the world who needed him. So he began to isolate himself more and more. We heard he was trying to sell his farm and livestock, but when we made an offer to buy them ourselves, he seemed distraught and unable to take a decision.'

'So,' Baz asked, 'the farm is not sold?'

'No,' she shook her head sadly. 'He has left all his affairs incomplete.'

'*Chachi*,' said Roopmati, '*Baba* was supposed to come and live with me in Mandu. Did he not tell you or *Chacha* about this?'

'No, *beta*, he did not say anything. If you ask me, I would say he had no intention of leaving his home ever. He may have agreed to your suggestion just to keep you happy, but I think he wanted to live here only.'

'And die here,' Baz added softly. 'Roopmati, I think it is well that he did what his heart wanted. He loved the river as much as you do and will be at peace once we let him merge into her waters.'

'Yes,' she whispered. 'The same waters in which my mother's and my grandparents' ashes were immersed. He will join them at last ... '

Early in the morning, the Narmada flowed from the rising sun like molten gold tipped from an alchemist's melting pot.

Roopmati tilted the clay pot with the ashes over the edge of the boat and watched them swirl and mingle with the fast flowing waters. She imagined her father meeting his loved ones at last and smiled, still holding the clay pot over the water.

Two strong hands came near her elbow and holding the pot, shook it until it was completely empty. Then they pointed to the water.

'Throw the pot in too.'

She turned to gaze into his face in wonderment.

He understands our rituals so well ... and he has been there for me today like a family member ... I can never forget this gesture of his, as long as I live.

She nodded and dropped the pot, and as it dipped and rocked in the waters, joined her hands in prayer.

Chapter 16

It was close to dusk as Roopmati and Baz walked their tired horses through the pathways of Mandu and stopped at the entrance of Shahi Mahal. The waiting stable hand leapt up to hold the Sultan's horse, but Baz curtly directed him to help with Roopmati's. Panna, who was playing dice with other servants under the trees, got up and heaving his breasts up with both hands, swayed his hips as he walked towards them, doing *aadaab*.

'Is this how you spend your time instead of doing your job guarding the mahal and running errands for Bibijaan and Sadiya?' The Sultan's tone was rough, but Panna only sniggered and hid his stubbled face in his sari *pallu*.

'This is your last warning, Panna. Next time I see or hear of your carelessness, you will be thrown out of Mandu before sunrise!'

They climbed the steps to the front door together. Roopmati turned to Baz and said, 'Thank you for everything you have done. Please go home and take some rest.' He nodded and continued to walk with her into the house. Sadiya was waiting at the entrance with her usual wide smile, her big kohl lined eyes warm and expressive. She bent low in greeting and then melted away.

They stood in the plushly carpeted audience hall, and there was a moment of awkward silence, then Baz spoke in a low voice.

'Roopmati, I understand your need to grieve, so I shall leave you alone until you send me a message.'

Flustered, Roopmati stammered, 'I ... I do not understand, *Huzoor* ... send you a message about what?' She could not believe that he expected her to make a romantic move towards him, to declare reciprocal feelings for him.

'About holding a *mehfil* of course,' he said softly, and smiled mischievously at her embarrassment. 'We have not had an evening together ever since that day when you were drenched in the rain and came to my palace.'

She flushed at the reminder.

'I ... I ... yes, we must have an evening of music soon. I will send word once I feel a little better.'

He bent his head and touched his fingertips to his brow.

'*Allah hafiz.*'

She watched him till he went down the steps then turned, startled at a sound behind her. Sadiya was holding a tray of refreshments.

'Bibijaan, I have brought you hot chai and kachoris. Will you have it here or in your chamber?' Her eyes were as clear and trusting as always. Roopmati felt a wave of contrition. She bent down and took the tray from her companion and placed it on a low table. Then she took Sadiya's tiny hands in hers and looked into her eyes.

'Sadiya, my dear friend, can you ever find the bigness of heart to forgive me?'

Sadiya shook her head and smiled her angelic smile.

'Bibijaan, you are shaming me by asking forgiveness. It is I who should have been more understanding, more sensitive of your feelings that day. I behaved like a caretaker, not a friend! I am sorry, Bibijaan!' Her eyes unexpectedly filled with tears.

Roopmati led her by the hand to a long low seat and coaxed her to sit down beside her. Sadiya wiped her eyes with the back of a hand and sniffled into her dupatta. 'You know, Bibijaan, I have never known what it is to have a family, nor even a close friend. When I was small, I was left in a masjid in Dhar by my parents as they knew I was not normal. Luckily, I was picked up by the Sultan's late mother who told everyone that she felt a strange connection with me. She brought me here to Mandu when I was four years old. I stayed in the servants' quarters, but since no one controlled me, I ran wild and did whatever I liked. I sat in the classrooms with the noblemen's children and learned Persian. This great language opened up for me the world of literature and theology and philosophy. I attended music lessons given to other children and my happiest hours were spent reading poetry and tuning musical instruments while other children played outside.'

She shook her head. 'I have no regrets that I could not run and play with them nor later, share their dreams and romantic interests. Perhaps,' she paused thoughtfully, 'my only dream was to have a family of my own one day. And that is what I have found after you came here. I think of you not just as my mistress, but also love you like a sister.'

Roopmati bent down and hugged Sadiya. They stayed like that, heart to heart, for a few moments, then with a choked laugh, Roopmati got up and wiped her tears.

'Well! That is a lot of emotions over two days, don't you think?' Both of them burst out laughing.

Roopmati finished her morning *riyaz* and put aside the tanpura, then turned, surprised, at the gruff sound of a man's voice behind her.

Panna stood in the room, moving his shoulders and tossing his head arrogantly.

Roopmati wondered what the Sultan would say if he saw him now.

'What is it, Panna?'

'There is a message for you from her royal highness, Sultana Hiba Rahima.'

Roopmati stood up, stunned. The Sultan's wife! What could she want with her? Never had she imagined herself meeting Hiba. Her heart thudded as another thought struck her. The Sultan had said he was estranged from her. Had the Sultana suspected that her *shauhar* was getting involved with his singer and decided to come and appraise this other woman, perhaps even have a showdown with her?

Panna continued.

'Begum Hiba sends her condolences on the death of your father and would like to come and express them to you personally. She wants to meet you tomorrow around noon.'

Well, I have not done anything wrong, not even in thought, so why should I be afraid? Let her come, I shall greet her with respect and honour ...

'Let her come. Thank you.'

Sadiya narrowed her eyes at the news. She was stitching pink and white fabric roses on to a dark blue sari for Roopmati to wear at a *mehfil* soon. She looked up and shook her head.

'I am afraid there is something suspicious here, Bibijaan.'

'Suspicious? What do you mean?

'Well, you do not know Hiba Begum, but I have seen her ever since she came here as the Sultana, 7 years ago. She is not, how do I say it, she is not very intelligent, nor even capable of thinking for herself!'

'Is she beautiful?' The words were out before she could stop them.

Sadiya paused and looked at her mistress thoughtfully, and then continued, 'Yes, she is very beautiful. Slim and shapely, with creamy skin and long black hair. But,' she shook her head, 'very little else to her. I doubt she held the Sultan's attention for very long after marriage, hence the long and endless line of women over the years.'

Roopmati walked restlessly to the window. She felt strangely annoyed. 'Sadiya, you were saying there is something suspicious, remember?'

'Yes, yes, Bibijaan, I am coming to it! Hiba Begum being, well, how she is, it is not likely that she would have herself thought of coming to pay her respects to you for your loss. Someone else has put her up to it, and I know exactly who it is!'

Roopmati frowned. What was Sadiya leading up to?

'Bibijaan, the Sultana's mother lives here in Mandu and she is, how do I say it, a very aggressive, interfering woman, always controlling her daughter. She must be behind this move.'

'But Sadiya, what could be suspicious about both of them wanting to pay me a condolence call?'

Sadiya laughed, a loud, deep throaty laugh.

'What indeed? Oh my dear Bibijaan, what indeed?'

~

They arrived in two palkis and were ushered into the public audience room by a grinning Panna.

Hiba was resplendent in a purple *sharara* shot through with pink and silver stars and heavy silver jewellery. Her long hair had been combed and left open in a cascade of curls down her back. Jana Begum was in an unrelenting brown burkha. She threw the veil back and examined the room and its furnishings, chewing slowly. Hiba bit her little finger nervously and twitched her nose like a rabbit. She couldn't wait to see Roopmati, and yet she wished her mother had not brought her here.

Sadiya made them comfortable and slipped into Roopmati's chamber.

'Bibijaan! Did I not tell you?' she whispered. 'The mother is here too! And she's examining our carpets and curtains!'

Roopmati looked amused and mystified. 'How ... what ... how does that matter? May be she is just fond of rich silks and embroidery work.'

'Or,' Sadiya lowered her voice and enunciated slowly, with a wicked gleam, 'maybe she's planning to have them removed so that you cannot have any more musical evenings there with her son-in-law!' She winked.

Roopmati entered the hall with her hands folded in a namaste. For a few seconds no one spoke as the three women sat and appraised each other. Then Jana Begum said, 'We are very sorry to hear about your father, Roopmati.'

Hiba immediately spoke up. 'Yes, may Allah grant peace to his soul.'

Roopmati bent her head in response.

There was another silence as refreshments were served. Jana Begum seemed to be formulating the right words in her mind.

'We hear my dear son-in-law-has been very kind to you. We hear he personally escorted you to your home to perform the last rites.'

'Yes.'

'Yes, he is a good man. He will do good for anyone who is in need. As the ruler of Malwa, there are many poor souls who have received his patronage and his timely help. You must be very grateful to him indeed.' Jana Begum shook her head sympathetically.

Roopmati hesitated, uncomfortable discussing her equation with the Sultan.

The older woman continued speaking, while Hiba sat playing with her black tresses and twisted a strand around her finger to admire it in the afternoon light that came in through the window.

'So what do you plan to do now? Are your farms sold or disposed of by your poor father?'

Roopmati felt the tears pricking her eyes. She shook her head wordlessly. At her elbow, she sensed Sadiya's sucked in breath and a warning pressure as she leaned against her.

'Oh? So they are still lying there, untended? What about your cattle?'

Roopmati moved uneasily. 'My uncle is now taking care of them,' she said biting her lip and looked at her hands lying in her lap.

Jana Begum clicked her tongue in concern. 'You must be waiting to move back to your home, dear child. No one is ever happy far from home. And I hear that you are very devoted to the Narmada river.' She leaned forward conspiratorially. 'The river always calls. Your heart will heal only when the pain is washed away by her waters.'

Sadiya suddenly spoke up.

'Oh no, Bibijaan sees her river every day. The Sultan has found a point high up near the wall from where she can have a darshan as well as do puja to the river mata.'

Jana Begum's nostrils flared as if she had smelt something bad. She stared at Sadiya unblinkingly.

'And,' continued Sadiya, 'why would Bibijaan move back to live in that house alone, when she can sing everyday with the Sultan, who, Allah praise him, has given her every comfort here?'

'Why indeed!' Jana said with a faint sneer and shifted her gaze back to Roopmati.

'Dear child, it must be lonely for you. Do come and visit us in the Sultana's royal palace sometimes. After all, as a musician, you have nothing else to keep you occupied after you do your daily practice, is it not?'

Sadiya made to speak again, but Jana Begum hastily turned to her daughter, 'Come, let us leave now. We have taken a lot of Roopmati's precious time, and it may start to rain soon!'

Chapter 17

He *was in a large room, a long, beautiful hall whose walls sloped upwards from the ground, a hall that was like a swing, a cradle that protected him. That is why he had no sense of danger. Then why did they all look so concerned—Mirza Faiz and Sahed Ali and Beg Khan and the rest?*

Surrounded by his courtiers, he looked around puzzled. Beg Khan spoke up, his voice distorting and echoing, his features twisting, warping in the dim dankness of the place.

In danger ... your brothers want to kill you ... fight them, exile them, protect your kingdom ...

His head ached and he longed to sit in his moonlit courtyard and pick on his been sitar *... music soothed all pains ... but they would not let him go. Suddenly, a thick arm came around his neck from behind and he twisted his arm back and slashed blindly with a dagger. The arm loosened and he heard a sickening thud, but no, he wouldn't turn, he did not want to know who he had killed, because he knew ... when it's your own blood, you always know ...*

Sobbing deep in his throat, his body slithery with sweat, Baz slowly came back to the sound of birds calling in the tree outside his window. He sat up, his breath still short and gasping.

When will my nightmares ever end? I did what I never wanted to do, all I wanted was Mandu. Abbujaan knew and gave me my pleasure capital but my brothers were not content with their own bequest ... Alas, they brought doom upon themselves, but I, I have to live with more than my inheritance, I have to wake and sleep and dream with my two demons ... the slaying of one brother and the exile of another.

Baz ran a hand over his face and cleared his throat.

'Come!' he called to the soft knock on his door.

How does this cursed man always know when I am awake? Does he wait with his ear to the door?

His manservant bowed low. His expression deadpan as ever.

'*Huzoor*, there is a messenger come to Mandu for you.'

'A messenger? From where?'

A faint gleam of excitement flickered over Ahmed's implacable countenance.

'From Agra, *Huzoor*.'

Baz threw off his sheets and stood up.

'From Agra!'

'Yes, Huzoor, from the court of Shahenshah Akbar.'

Baz stared at the man unbelievingly.

'From Padshah Akbar! And you stand here as calm as a Sufi saint, giving me the news as if you are bringing me a message from the Sultana's mother!'

His master's mixed metaphors notwithstanding, Ahmed bowed his head and waited for permission to continue.

'Well? Are you now going to stand silently? Do you not understand how important this could be?'

'Huzoor, the messenger arrived in the early hours of the morning, riding almost without a stop on the way. I sent him to eat, drink and rest awhile. Besides, I did not want to disturb your sleep when you could well be informed in the morning.'

'Hmm. I will receive the messenger in my court at the Hindola Mahal in an hour's time. Prepare my bath, lay out my formal *chogha* and ceremonial pagri and patka.'

As Baz rode his horse fitted with a gold braided bridle and a tasselled, richly embroidered blanket over which sat the burnished leather saddle, he wondered yet again what Emperor Akbar could possibly want with him.

Does he want my help with troops in his upcoming campaigns in Rajputana? Does he want information about the territories of Ahmad Shah in Gujarat? Does he, perhaps, wish to invite me to his court in Agra as a sign of friendship?

The kingdom of Malwa had not had any discord, military or diplomatic, with the Mughal forces since Emperor Humayun had conquered the Mandu fort two decades ago. Since then, much had ensued. Mandu had been taken by Sher Shah Suri who appointed his general Shujaat Khan as Governor in Malwa. With the decline in Sher Shah's fortunes, Shujaat Khan, father of Baz Bahadur, had declared himself as independent ruler. But he did not live long after that. He died leaving Baz as the new Sultan of Malwa.

And in Agra a new Mughal ruler sits on the throne, Akbar. We have no enmity with him. So perhaps, this is Akbar's hand of friendship that he now extends to me for future alliances.

Baz was smiling when he walked into the Hindola Mahal preceded by a flourish of trumpets and an announcement by the chief guard.

As he took his place on the indigo velvet lined regal chair, he looked down the rows of courtiers on both sides, all of them bent and frozen in *aadaab* postures. Behind them, the walls of the Hindola Mahal sloped gently upwards, giving the impression that the long hall was a swing, a cradle. Then he looked up at the gallery, where the women were gathered to quietly watch the court proceedings. Among the veiled faces, he recognised the brown burkha of Jana Begum and the kohl lined eyes of Hiba. In vain, he scanned the other covered faces, hoping to see Roopmati there, even though he knew in his heart that she would never come unless invited by him.

'*Aadaab.*' He returned the courtiers' greetings, sat down and raised his hands asking them to be seated too.

'The court has gathered today to receive a messenger from the court of Mughal Padshah Akbar at Agra. We will listen to him speak, and then discuss what the message means to us at Malwa.'

He raised his hand to a guard at the back of the hall and watched a well-dressed man stride forward escorted by two guards. He stopped in front of Baz, removed his feathered cap and bowed very low.

'Speak. What brings you here to Mandu, the jewel of Malwa?'

'Huzoor, I come as a messenger of no less than Shahenshah Abu'l-Fath Jalal-ud-din Muhammad Akbar himself, scion of the great line of Mughals, who trace their lineage from the warrior dynasty of Genghis Khan and Timur the Great. As third in line after the Emperors of Hindustan, Babur and Humayun, Padsha Akbar commands territories as far as the mind can envisage. He truly lives up to his title, Ruler of the World.'

Baz nodded.

'Tell me your mission.'

'As you must have heard, the Shahenshah is a patron of the fine arts, music, literature, painting and sculpture. His court echoes with the sweet sound of raga and *alaap*, and rings with the beat of tablas and the chime of *ghungroos*. The greatest artistes of the world perform in the Mughal court and are cherished by the Emperor like precious pearls on a string around his neck.' He paused.

Baz was intrigued where this was leading. He stroked his jaw and raised a hand encouragingly.

'Go on.'

'Huzoor, gifted musicians are like glowing lamps. They cannot be hidden from the world for long. Mian Tansen's fame has spread from the court of Raja Ramchandra Singh of Rewa in Central Hindustan. You yourself are renowned in Lahore, Dilli, Agra, where they speak of your Bazkhani style of singing. And now,' he paused for effect, 'now, the Emperor is ready to discover a new talent. From your own realm.' He bowed dramatically.

There was a long silence. Baz gazed at the top of the man's head. His mind was suddenly blank.

'I speak of the new voice in your court, of course. A young woman by the name of Roopmati.'

Baz felt the blood rush to his head. He half rose, then sank back in his seat at a cautioning look from Mirza Faiz on his right side.

'Huzoor, may I read out this letter from Adham Khan Saheb, *sipahsalar* and closest confidante of the Emperor, written on his behalf?'

He waited a few seconds, but seeing no response on the Sultan's face, unfurled the cloth banner and began to read.

As-Salaam-Alaikum. *By this letter sent through the messenger of the Mughal court, I, Adham Khan, Chief of His Emperor's armies, greet you, Miyan Bayazid Baz Bahadur Khan, Sultan of Malwa, and wish you good health and success in all your endeavours. I write this letter on behalf of Shahenshah Jalaluddin Akbar the First.*

The court of Mandavgarh is renowned for its patronage of music among other fine arts. It has come to the ears of the Emperor that there is a new voice in your midst, a maiden by the name of Roopmati who has surpassed all standards of excellence in her talent, knowledge and rendition of the classical form. As you know, the Emperor gathers in his court the very best exponents of music, dance, literature and art.

Artistes from every corner of Hindustan consider themselves fortunate to be handpicked to perform in the Mughal court.

I hereby request that the maiden Roopmati be immediately sent to the court of Shahenshah Akbar, wherein she will be treated with honour and respect, the only expectation from her being to perform for His Majesty and his coterie of nobles, whenever his royal highness desires. Awaiting your assent and thereby your acceptance of the Mughal dynasty's hand of friendship and support.

The silence in the hall was complete; everyone held their breath as they looked towards the Sultan on his indigo velvet chair.

Suddenly, like a clap of thunder, Baz slapped his hands down on the smooth teakwood arms and jumped up. He pointed a hard forefinger at the messenger and flicked it.

'Out!' he said in a tone that picked up the pitch of the air inside the Hindola Mahal and reverberated through the hall. 'Out!'

The messenger remained standing, unfazed.

'Is this the final message I take back to the Shahenshah's *sipahsalar*, Adham Khan?'

Baz narrowed his blazing eyes and called out, 'Koi hai?'

The court watched in fascinated horror as the messenger from the court of Shahenshah Akbar, Emperor of Hindustan, was ignominiously led out by guards.

~

In the gallery above, the women waited until the Sultan, and then all the noblemen had filed out of the Hindola Mahal.

Then Jana Begum turned to her daughter and threw back her veil.

'So! It is now time to action the next part of my plan. Roopmati must go, and go she will.'

Chapter 18

Striding out of the Hindola Mahal, his personal guards hurrying behind him, Baz pulled off his turban and threw it down, then raising a hand to the men to leave him alone, leapt onto his horse and galloped away. He skirted the Suraj Talab towards the western boundary of the city where the plateau curved sharply inwards, dropping steeply down sheer rock faces on the outer side. He finally stopped near the Lohani Caves and leaving his horse to graze in the grassy meadows, walked up to a rocky outcrop and sat down. Here the fort walls had been worn down by the strong winds from the ravines and were just a jagged line of broken rocks.

Close to the sheer chasm formed to the west of the Mandu plateau, he gazed at the awe-inspiring splendour of the gorges lying before him and listened to the howl and whoop of the winds. It was the sound of his boyhood, when he had often ridden out here to be alone. Picking on the strings of his *been sitar* he would try to match the *shruti* of his instrument to the pitch of the winds. Every sound of nature had always seemed to have the notes of music in them. The pleading call of the koel, the gush of monsoon streams, even the harsh cry of the peacock.

After some time, Baz felt a sense of peace seep into his soul. His anger ebbed away and he looked around, soaking in the spectrum of greens, from the barely discernible tinge in the rainwater puddles around, to the dark mossy clumps on the rocks, to the bright green of parrots as they shot across the sky in formation.

He laughed. He would bring Roopmati here, to his favourite hideaway, and they would enjoy the beauty of the hills together. She was a girl born and raised in the plains, but he would make her forget those grasslands and rivers and sheesham and sal forests, and get her captivated by this, his land, his Mandu, where everything was larger than life. The colours, the sounds, the sweeping vistas of hills and valleys and ravines and ridges.

We will sit here on these rocks and then perhaps it will rain and I will pull her into one of the caves where sodden to the skin, we will study the sculptures of Hindu gods and goddesses together.

Suddenly, he was aroused. He had seen her drenched to the skin before and he could remember every curve, every outline of her body. He often imagined himself unwinding her sari, deliberately, all six yards of it, then gazing at her in her blouse and petticoat. He would peel, yes, slowly peel away the wet blouse, his eyes never leaving the dark shadows in front that pushed against the fabric so tantalisingly. But by the time he had undressed her, she would always be frustratingly covered again in her abundant tresses. Swathing herself with her long wet hair, she would look at him defiantly.

'I am not one of your concubines,' she would tell him. 'Don't you dare touch me.'

I want to touch you, Roopmati. And not just touch you, I want to do so much more to you. But I have given my word of honour, so I cannot make a move on you. It will have to be you who approaches me. You will have to come to me with love, with desire ...

'Roopmati! I am waiting for you!' He shouted, turning all around, his arms thrown out and face raised to the falling drops. His voice was whipped away by the gradually speeding winds.

No Hindustan ka Padsha, no Shahenshah, has any right to so much as look at her, leave aside listen to her sing or have her adorn his court. Roopmati is mine, and only mine.

On a sudden whim, he ran lightly to his horse, and leaping onto the saddle, kicked its flanks and, began to gallop towards the palace complex. He needed to see Roopmati again. It had been more than 15 hours.

~

Roopmati was laughing so hard that her stomach hurt. Sadiya was imitating Jana Begum and her daughter by turns.

First she stared silently at Roopmati with her nostrils twitching, then pretended to take out a paan from her *paan daan* and stuff it into her mouth. She then flicked her head to one side and spoke indistinctly through a full mouth.

'Daughter, this woman needs to go back to her sheep. What do you say?'

Sadiya suddenly became Hiba. She widened her eyes, clapped her hands to her cheeks and bleated nervously. The impersonated Jana Begum turned to her impatiently.

'No, no, I don't mean say something to the sheep! You silly girl, you look like one yourself!'

'Stop!' Roopmati held her sides, her eyes streaming.

But Sadiya was in full form and refused to stop. She continued with her little charades and the hall rang with peals of laughter. In the middle of a giggle, Roopmati glanced towards the doorway, suddenly stopped and scrambled to her feet, gathering her long open tresses together at the back in a knot.

'Do not rise, please,' Baz's voice was deep and gentle. He walked into the hall and she noticed that although he was formally attired, his hair was windblown and there was drying black mud on his boots.

Sadiya sidled out of the room, shooting significant looks at her mistress through her big kohl-lined eyes.

What is she trying to convey? This Sadiya is too much! First she makes me laugh uncontrollably, and now sends some secret messages! I am not even going to try to understand them.

Unaware that her face was flushed and her eyes bright, Roopmati took a deep breath and indicated a seat.

'Huzoor, will you be seated?'

'No, I will not sit. I came ... I came ...' For the first time in his adult life, Baz Bahadur, the Sultan of Malwa, was at a loss for words.

'I came to ask if you have recovered yet from the death of your father, but,' he raised a hand as she opened her lips to speak, 'I realise how insensitive that sounds. What I truly do mean, is that if you sing, you may express your feelings and feel better.'

'Huzoor, I think nothing could be more wrong than to call you insensitive. You have been not just very generous and kind, but the greatest support I could ask for in my circumstances. I ... I wish to thank you from my heart.'

Baz shook his head self-deprecatingly.

But I want your heart, Roopmati.

'Huzoor, I think I am ready to sing today. My dear friend Sadiya has lightened my mood considerably with her antics.'

'But there will be no *mehfil*. It will be only you and me. I wish to read some of my poetry to you in private.'

She nodded, her eyes sparkling.

'And I mine to you.'

'Till dusk, then.'

He put his hand on his heart and looked at her, then bowed and strode out.

~

Till dusk then.

Roopmati sat by the window of the audience hall, her heartbeat uneven. She bit her lower lip hard, willing herself to stay calm. Outside, Mandu was slowly dissolving into the grey tones of evening; she knew that like the dark *amavasya* night that would light up with diyas and crackers on Diwali, Mandu nights too started deceptively dark before bursting into lights and sounds that would carry on until the sun rose again.

Suddenly, she knew she could not be alone with the Sultan tonight. There was something in his eyes that made her feel all warm and quivery; it made her feel that her body, her thoughts, were not in her control any more.

'Sadiya!' She called.

Where is Sadiya when I need her here? And what was she trying to convey to me earlier this evening with her meaningful expressions?

Sadiya had taken out a pale pink cotton sari and matched it with a black blouse with a woven border in pink and cream thread. She had plaited her mistress's long hair into braids and wound them around her head, fastening them in place with silver pins. Silver *jhumkas* set with pink sapphires swung from her ears. Sadiya had left her neck bare, allowing the black blouse to pick out the creamy tones of her skin. As she touched her pulse spots with sandal paste, Sadiya smiled mysteriously. Roopmati caught the look in the mirror.

'Sadiya! Why do you smile? What is it? What goes on in your mind? This is just like any other evening, you know! The Sultan is ...'

'Shh, Bibijaan, I think I hear the clatter of hooves! Perhaps he is here!'

That was just a ruse to get me to stop asking questions. Wait until I get her alone again tomorrow ...

She quickly turned from the window and looked towards the doorway at the sound of a soft cough.

'Bibijaan, the Sultan is here.' Panna lowered his eyes. But his jaw was hard and set.

She nodded at the eunuch and stood up, glancing towards her notebook on the low table. There were all her thoughts, her poems, her random jottings of the last few months, written in chaste Brijbhasha, the language of her learning. Yes, she was ready to share her art with the Sultan, but not her heart.

Much, much later, as the night sky became unrelentingly dark and the lights in the waters of Munj Talab dissipated in the falling rain, Roopmati sat by the window again. Her mind was replete with words and images and the sound of Baz reading a poem written in the simple *khariboli* that he favoured.

'It is about the festival of Holi,' he had explained and read out from his book ...

Dampati khelat hors mahal men
Sobha barni na jai
Sakuch chhar ang ang liptane,
saras mate douw
Baz Bahadur fagua saras machai

She nodded and paraphrased softly, 'The couple sprinkles coloured water in the palace, the beauty of which scene cannot be described. Abandoning modesty they clasp body to body, both intoxicated with mirth. Baz Bahadur celebrates the spring festival merrily.' The picture that rose to her mind made her insides tingle not unpleasantly.

He explained, 'Here in Mandu, we celebrate the festival to welcome spring as much as you all do in the plains. Like the divine couple Radha and Krishna, we spray coloured water and throw clouds of coloured powder on one another, tie *ghungroo*s on our ankles and dance with abandon, then make love under the trees and behind the rose bushes. What better time to express our attraction for one another than while intoxicated with bhang, and with wet clothes clinging to our bodies?'

His smiling eyes had lingered on her face, then moved down, flicking over her curves barely discernible beneath the sari. Roopmati had hastily picked up her notebook and flipping it open, read out the first poem that she saw there.

Afterwards, the talk had veered to Sufi poetry and its rendition in musical forms.

'What do you think of the Sufi thinkers and poets?' he asked. 'Chisti, Rumi, Hafez ... I for one have been greatly influenced by their art. There is a truth in it that reaches out to me. Call it universal truth, or call it music that vibrates with our soul, I am deeply affected by Sufi lyrics and by the ghazal form of music.'

She considered. 'Huzoor, I am trained in the Dhrupad style, which is based on the devotional music traditionally performed in Hindu temples. This form of music expresses the bhakti rasa. Meerabai sang bhajans to Krishna in the bhakti tradition.'

Baz raised a mischievous eyebrow.

'For every Meerabai there were a hundred *gopis* professing romantic love for Krishna, were there not?'

She shook her head seriously.

'Huzoor, that was just maya. We believe that each of the *gopis* was so drunk with devotion for Krishna that He made her believe that He belonged to her alone. Hence the illusion each *gopi* had of dancing exclusively with Him in the forests of Brindavan.'

'Hmm. But you have not said anything about setting Sufi poetry to music and of singing ghazals!'

'Huzoor ... I think I am too much of a purist; in my Guru's musical tradition, singing ghazals would be considered a ... sacrilege.'

Baz gave a chuckle. 'Sacrilege!'

She nodded sincerely. 'Yes. Sufi and ghazal themes centre around romantic love, separation, pining for the beloved, mystical reflection ... the shringara rasas as we call them. These are frivolous themes that may be dealt with in poetry, but never in the classical music I practise.' She touched her ears reverently. 'My guru taught me to regard my music as a god, not something to be played around with.'

'Ah!' he smiled and raised a long forefinger. 'But if you say your music is your God, then surely your music should be as playful as Krishna with the *gopis*! Or as varied as the avatars of Vishnu. Did he not change himself in every *yug* of human history?'

She gazed at him wide-eyed.

He can talk about my religion as if he truly knows ...

'Huzoor, your arguments are very persuasive! But I remain unconvinced. Musical traditions do not change with the times. I prefer to sing Hindustani music in its pure form.'

He gave his special, crooked smile.

'Interesting! Would that be because pure Hindustani music centres on the Hindu gods as subjects, and ghazals stem from Islamic mysticism?' He raised an eyebrow at her.

She sucked in her breath.

'Of course not, Huzoor! I am shocked that you should think so! You know as well as I do that art has no religion, and music knows no creed! I may say that music is my God, but it is a god only in being so perfect, so complete, that we as singers aspire to become a part of it, but never to create a self-serving aura around it!'

He nodded, impressed by her thinking. 'Yes, I agree with you. Music is universal, it reaches for that inner core of us, rather than outward to any god. To that extent, I would say that it is a spiritual experience.'

She nodded thoughtfully. He had expressed it so well.

Baz continued. 'I have great respect for your worship of the elements—the sun and the forests and the rivers, because it is nature that resonates with our soul. And strangely, when I listen to you sing, I am reminded of creation. It is as if I can feel the cool breeze on my face and hear music in the sounds of nature. In fact, I too write my poems sitting in the forest, not in the confines of my palaces that are heavy with the scents of *ittar* and surrounded by velvet drapes. Too much softness suffocates me, you know.'

For the first time, Roopmati forgot her shyness and looked back into his eyes and nodded eagerly.

'And I have always been inspired by my river. I write and sing by her music. Even in my home, even at night, even in my dreams, her sounds never leave me.'

The evening ended when Baz looked out of the window at the glow of Mandu gradually dimming with the extinguishing of her lamps. There was a guarded eagerness, a watchful anticipation on his face, as he took his leave of her.

'You look very beautiful in cotton saris. They give you much grace and charm. But perhaps some day, you will consent to wear a lehenga-choli like the women here do.'

She widened her eyes and shook her head laughingly.

'Oh, I do think the women look very beautiful in their heavily worked lehengas and diaphanous dupattas! But I wear one? Oh no! I don't think I could ever carry off one of those! Only simple cotton neevi or saris for me.'

He bent his head and touched his fingertips to his brow.

'*Allah hafiz*,' he said and was gone.

Chapter 19

Under the evening sky, the Yamuna was a silvery grey ribbon that had been unfurled carelessly by the gods dwelling in the Himalayas and left to cascade down the plains. From the highest point on the fort, the wind-blown open terrace enclosed by battlements, the river looked strangely insignificant, just a stray thread in the vast, awe-inspiring fabric of the Empire.

But Abu'l-Fath Jalal-ud-din Muhammad Akbar, monarch of all he surveyed, knew better. As he walked ruminatively on the red stone floor and paused at the end of each round at the parapet walls, he looked down at the river and thanked her silently for the prosperity and well being of his capital city, Agra. He thought of his grandfather, Babur, who had chosen to make this his capital when he conquered Hindustan and his father, Humayun, who would have been standing here as the Emperor if he had not died so tragically and so young.

This was Akbar's quiet time of the day, when he needed to be alone to think and plan and reflect; he left his bodyguards on the steps below with strict instructions not to disturb him unless it was absolutely necessary.

It was two years since Akbar had sat on the Mughal throne; two years of consolidating his position that had been challenged by Hemu, the fiery general of Adil Shah Suri, whom he had defeated in a glorious battle. Now at last, he could breathe free and plan fresh campaigns to spread his empire in all directions. With Gwalior recently overpowered, he could look towards the conquest of Rajputana and Gujarat to the west, Gondwana in central Hindustan and Bengal to the east. In fact, he needed to call his council to meet the very next morning. No time could be wasted in the pursuit of his dream, his destiny ...

I need to embed the name of my Gurkhani lineage that Hindustan refers to as the Mughal dynasty, in the memory of the world, ever to be remembered as the greatest empire that ever existed.

There was the sound of raised voices and the crash of boots on the staircase. He turned and saw his *sipahsalar*, Adham Khan, swagger on to the terrace. Faintly annoyed, Akbar raised his eyebrows at his commander-in-chief who was also his milk brother, having been suckled as infants by the same woman, Adham's mother, Maham Aga.

'Well, Adham? What is this urgent matter that causes you to disturb me in my quiet hour?'

Adham gave an insolent smile. Here, by themselves, they were not ruler and subject, but peers.

'Jalal, you will not take this sarcastic tone of voice when you learn that you have been insulted in public.'

Akbar continued standing with his hands behind his back, waiting for Adham to explain. There was no change in his expression.

'Jalal, do you remember that I had told you of a singer of note in the court of the Malwa Sultanate? On hearing of this woman named Roopmati, I had recommended that you acquire her for your court, to add to your collection of artistes and poets. You had agreed and asked me to send a message to Sultan Baz Bahadur on your behalf.'

'Well?'

'Well, the Sultan has unequivocally refused to send the singer to you and has had the messenger thrown out in front of all the nobles and counsels!'

There was a short silence while Akbar looked thoughtfully at his milk brother.

'Hmm ... yes, Baz Bahadur has behaved not just emotionally, but also foolishly. Perhaps he is in love with the woman.'

Adham almost sputtered in exasperation.

'What? Are you insane? The man has insulted you, Jalal! He needs to be punished.'

'And how do you propose we do that?'

'I must take my armies and wage war on him!'

'Hmm. Perhaps. But again, perhaps that would be an over-reaction. Adham, remember, there are more important states to conquer and bigger enemies to vanquish. In fact, the council shall meet tomorrow to plan our next campaign. Music, art and literature are important to our court, but conquered territories are important to the building of our empire. So let this go now.'

'I shall not forget this insult, Jalal! It shall be avenged some day.'

Akbar put a hand on Adham's shoulder and nodded with a smile.

'Of course it shall, my milk brother. Go now in peace.'

Four hundred miles away, to the south-west of Agra, in the hill fortress of Mandu, in Jal Mahal, the palace of the Sultana, Hiba lay on her bed sobbing. Panna stood nearby, twisting his sari pallu nervously.

'Begum Saheba, please forgive me! I have brought you bad news indeed! But it was the instructions of your mother, Jana Begum, that I tell you both about every single meeting between the ... *huh* ... singing woman,' his face twisted in a grimace, 'and the Sultan!'

'Did you tell *Ammi*?' Hiba raised her swollen face.

'Yes, I did tell her just now, that the Sultan and that woman spent most of last night alone together.'

'And what did *Ammi* say?'

Panna put a forefinger to his stubbled chin and thought, swaying all the time.

'Ahh! I remember now! She told me to tell you!'

'Fool! Go away! You are jesting with me.'

Panna looked around uncertainly, then deciding to take the Sultana's words at face value, slipped out of the heavy half-open doors, his broad shoulders almost getting stuck between them.

Hiba sat up and wiping her face with a muslin towel, blew her nose into it, then threw it on the floor. She clapped for her maidservant.

'Tell *Ammi* to come here immediately.'

'Abbi?' The woman asked with a puzzled expression. She stared at Hiba's face and hoarse voice; she was new and unaware of her mistress's temper tantrums. She was caught unawares when a moment later a silver nut bowl crashed into her chest.

Hiba watched her run out of the room, then got out of bed and sat by the window to wait for her mother.

Jana Begum walked in as usual, sliding between the doors as quiet as a cat, and seating herself opposite her daughter, began to make herself a paan. Hiba watched her through the whole process, breathing hard to stop herself from screaming out. Finally she asked in a trembling voice, 'So, what is it to be? Will that ... that whore replace me as the Sultana? Will she lie with my Baz, ride with him, sing with him, even bear him fine sons? What is it to be, *Ammi,* tell me, and what is going to happen to me then?' With a loud whoop, she burst into tears again.

Jana Begum raised the folded green leaf triangle to her mouth, then changed her mind and lowered it again.

'You, my daughter, are more foolish than I thought. It is the Shahid Khan family's blood in your veins of course! Your father too was like this! And his brothers and their father before that. *Humphh*! That day, in the Hindola Mahal, I told you that I have a new plan.'

'Plans, plans, plans! I am tired of all your plotting with nothing coming out of it! Your message to Adham Bhai in Agra to get the woman there! Your trying to convince the woman to return to the plains! Nothing worked!' She clicked her fingers in front of her mother's face, her pretty features distorted in a petulant sneer. 'And do you think Baz insulting the messenger will make the emperor send out an army here? Not a chance!'

Jana Begum shook her head. 'No, the Mughal army has much bigger enemies to fight.'

'So! You admit we have lost!'

'Ah, and that is where you are not just foolish, but impatient too!' The older woman leaned forward, her face set with determination. 'I have been a chess player in my time. A great champion! While the other women sat around in the *zananakhana* to gossip or play dice or just to beautify themselves, I would play chess with Panna's uncle, also a eunuch. Lolo, he was called. Dark-skinned, thickset, pock-marked, but with a brilliant mind. Lolo had picked up the game in his youth, while watching over Fana Sahib, a nobleman, as his personal bodyguard. Fana Sahib had no interest in women, you know, or for that matter, in men. He was known to be a neuter in his body but obsessed with its safety, and hence the bodyguard. He spent all his evenings over a chess board, playing with anyone who was interested. Sometimes, he would play against himself if he had no opponent! While other men drank and sang and danced and took lovers, he sat all night playing chess.'

'*Ammi*, where are you going with all this?'

'Again impatience! So, Lolo learnt the game just by watching. He would often come to the women's quarters late at night while his master slept, to spend time with us, and we became friendly. He taught me chess, which has in turn taught me patience, strategy and tactics. So,' she sat back with her first smile in weeks, displaying a set of brown uneven teeth.

'So, I have now planned to oust Roopmati by playing the game of strategy.'

Hiba's breathing had slowed by now. She spoke more calmly, 'Tell me.'

'Alright. Based on my knowledge of my nephew's character, I plan to create a situation which will solve the problem by itself. We will not need to get our hands dirty at all. Adham has a great weakness for women. And Roopmati is a very beautiful woman.' She ignored Hiba's whimper of protest. 'So I propose to show him what he is missing in his harem. Our court painter shall be commissioned to make a portrait of Roopmati which will be despatched to Adham Khan without delay. Then all we have to do is wait for the bugles and trumpets of the Mughal army at our gates.'

There was a long silence as Hiba assimilated the idea. Then she spoke out in a small voice.

'But how will you convince Roopmati to have her portrait painted? I cannot see her ever agreeing to it.'

'Ah ... your first intelligent question, Allah be praised! Leave that to me. We will both go and visit Roopmati in her palace tomorrow morning.'

Chapter 20

Against the darkness of the night skies, starlight hidden behind storm-laden clouds, rose the ship, a-sail on the high seas. Jahaz Mahal. Its open windows blazed with lights, its wide decks rang to the sounds of music and laughter and the halls within to the beat of *ghungroos* and tablas. Outside, the dark waters, where the vessel admired its own reflection, shimmered quietly, awaiting a storm. Baz looked up at the Jahaz Mahal and paused by the entrance at the centre of its long, sculpted frontage. His companions turned to him and laughed. One of them slapped Baz on the shoulder.

'Come, Baz, why this hesitation? You know you need this after a long, long time! How long have you been pining for this woman? Two months, three months?' Baz shook his head and ignored their teasing. They were his oldest companions, noblemen's sons he had grown up with. To them, he was not always the Sultan of Malwa, but a childhood playmate. For years, they had gone hunting and sailing, cockfighting and camel-racing together. And together they had drunk deep of the famed nightlife of Mandu, coming to the Jahaz Mahal night after night, to sing and dance, drink and smoke, and to finally wake up in a concubine's arms the next morning.

Now Baz looked at the lights and colourful figures visible at the windows and gestured to his companions to go on ahead.

'Come, Baz, celibacy is not a healthy state of body! It leads to insanity, they say!'

They elbowed each other into the doorway in a roar of bawdy jokes and laughter.

Baz turned and walked along the edge of the Kapur Talab that fronted the Jahaz Mahal and was presently a black mirror to its glory by night. He was disturbed and restless. Ever since he had expressed his feelings to Roopmati, he felt raw and exposed, super-sensitive to her every look and mood. He was also painfully aware that the promise he had made to himself was becoming more and more difficult to keep.

I have vowed that I will never force Roopmati to submit to me. She must come to me herself in love and in passion. But she is a fiercely independent woman, and one to whom her body is not as important as her music, nor indeed as her soul. I cannot entice her with silks and jewels and comforts. And although she feels our mutual attraction too, she will not surrender to the physical. Oh Roopmati, how shall I win you, your heart, your body, your soul?

There was a burst of clapping and applause from the central hall within. The *mujras* were about to begin. Suddenly weary of his own pining sadness, Baz walked to the doorway and made his entrance.

He stood at the door of the imposing hall of Jahaz Mahal, arms on his hips, and took in the scene. The centre of the marble stone floor had been cleared and it shone in polished splendour. Overhead, a crystal chandelier had been lit to resemble a gigantic diamond with shards of light reflecting off its myriad faces. The ceiling was looped with satin drapes in red and gold interspersed with long hanging strips of gold tinsel that spiralled whisperingly in the breezes that blew in.

The hall was laid out with rich carpets in red and gold, scattered with velvet cushions and bolsters. The men sprawled on the carpets and behind them, leaning against the walls, were attractive young women, dressed in silks and satins, and ready to cater to their slightest whims.

Seeing the Sultan, all the men stood up and bowed low over their hands. The women swayed forward, coquettishly smiling and fluttering kohl-lined eyes at him.

Aadaab ... aadaab ...

A voluptuous young woman stood in the middle of the hall in the classic pose at the start of a dance performance, her foot keeping time to the beat of the tabla. She shimmered in green silk and paisley brocade, her low-cut choli revealing a deep cleavage and her transparent *chunari* barely concealing her midriff. The tabla suddenly picked up tempo and the sarangi began to play a racy rendition of a ghazal. A man in a white kurta and colourful skull cap began to sing. As the dancer held up one end of her skirt, the other arm by her side, and began her intricate footwork, Baz raised his hands and the men sank to the floor again. He waited until more girls joined the dancer on the floor and the hall echoed to cries of *wah, wah* and coins began to clatter on the marble, then turned to slip away. Avoiding one end of the hall, where the terrace projected under the open sky, he walked to the other end. He had no interest in walking out into the bevy of girls who would be draped around the tortoise-shaped pool, their feet dipped in the slow flowing water, chattering and laughing as they waited for the men to come out for a round of ganja and the occasional bloody duel. He climbed the steps to the floor above, wondering where Saina was.

Saina had been his favourite though not his exclusive concubine. Beautiful in an aggressive kind of way, with big eyes, thick lips and ample shoulders, she satisfied not just his physical cravings, but also his need to be understood. Night after night, she had held him when he woke trembling from a nightmare and soothed him with gentle caresses, arousing him again, and making him roll around with her on the mattress with even more energy and aggression until finally shuddering to a stop, he would fall into a deep, dreamless sleep.

As Baz reached the open terrace his breath was snatched away by the cool breeze whipping up to precede a storm that would perhaps break after midnight. He walked along the edge of the terrace, looking down at the Munj Talab behind the Jahaz Mahal, and towards the Shahi Mahal beyond it. There was a dim light visible inside. He wondered if Roopmati was sitting by the window and looking towards him. A wave of longing washed over him. In despair, he looked up at the pitch black sky and quoted softly from his own poem:

Karta tumko kini sub layak
Meri mushkil karo asan
Jo jo tohe tak abay,
Man ichha phal pabay

'Oh Creator, I have made thee my judge, thou easest my hardships; whoever looks to thee, thou fulfillest his desire ...'

A sliver of lightning glanced through the sky. Baz gave a short laugh and lifted a hand to the heavens. As he walked around the terrace, ruminating on a new piece, the water gurgled in the channels along the edges, flowing from the Persian wheels that brought it up from the lake below. The channels took the water to the end of the terrace, to a lotus-shaped bath, slowing down through a maze to drop softly in, filling it, then down to the terrace below, to the tortoise-shaped pool where the girls lounged. From there, it would flow down into the underground reservoir, connected to the lakes.

He walked over to the sunken lotus bath barely discernible in the darkness. This was his private bathing area and no one else was allowed there without his command. He would often sit in the rose-scented waters when in pensive mood.

In the dimness of the terrace, he stripped and stepped into the water. Then sensed, rather than felt a bare body near him.

'Huzoor, you have come to me after so long! I am ready for you.' Saina's voice was thick and low, evocative of her attractions.

Baz turned and looked at her fully. She sat on the narrow ledge that ran along the sides, below the water surface. As his eyes got accustomed to the dimness, he saw her pale curves swaying in the water and knew that she wore nothing more than a string of sweet smelling mogra around her plump wrist.

She smiled through red, pouting lips and nodded her head enticingly.

In spite of his self imposed celibacy for months, in spite of being alone with a naked woman who had given him many a good time in bed over the years, Baz was cold to her attempts to seduce him. He could only think of Roopmati. Her slender beauty, her flawless skin and long wavy tresses, her eyes as large and shy as a doe's and her complete ignorance of her own charms. He nodded and smiled at Saina with an effort.

'Saina,' he said, then cleared his throat and started again. 'Saina, thank you for this er, surprise. I really appreciate it. But today, I am really not in the mood.'

She bit her lip coyly. 'Oh, Huzoor! You know Saina can change your mood easily! You know she has magic in her hands ...' She lifted her ringed fingers to tease her open lips.

Baz nodded again with a dry smile.

'Yes, I do Saina. But I think today I would like to be alone.'

He felt a hand snaking over his thigh under the water, He grabbed it and firmly removed it.

'Saina, it is now time for you to go. I want to be left alone.'

She batted her eyes at him, lips pouting in disappointment, then climbed out of the bath and picking up her clothes, melted into the darkness.

Baz lay back in the cool water and wondered what had happened to him. He could not concentrate on anything for long, he could not sleep, and now he could not even respond to a woman's body.

Except one. Roopmati's.

The night sky had turned a pale golden by the time Baz dressed to go down again. The clamour of voices from the tortoise pool directly below him had muted and he knew that all the bathing girls would have been picked up by the nobles and courtiers and would now be tangled in bed sheets with them. As he walked down the steps to the mighty hall below, there were snatches of music, but very desultory ... as if the player's heart was not in it anymore. After all, thought Baz, the music and dance here were not for the love of the arts, but only as a means to an end. Every night would start with enticing beats and voluptuous dancing to get the men in the mood. And excited men always pay well for the drinks and the opiates and the women.

The hall looked like the aftermath of an orgy; men and women were draped over the carpets and cushions, deep in languorous, drugged sleep. Some of the drapes and tinsel spirals had been pulled down from the ceiling. The tiered chandelier sported dark patches where the lamps had been snuffed out by enthusiastic pitching of *joothies* and caps in the air.

It's a wonder this place does not catch fire every night. I cannot believe I have been one of these senseless beings, dropping down on the floor night after night in a drunken stupor or into a harlot's arms.

He stood for a few minutes, studying the scene with a half smile. These revelers were not likely to be up and about in a hurry. The days began late in Mandu.The sun would be almost overhead by the time the roads and bazaars hummed to life. Streets of vendors hawking colourful clothes and jewellery and sweetmeats and carpets, embroiderers stretching silks over their wooden frames, the quilt-maker starting the *twang twang* of his *ruidhunai* to fluff cottonwool for the coming winters. Yes, it would be much, much later that the people would begin to come out and start their work.

While Mandu slept, one woman across the Munj Talab, Baz knew, would be freshly bathed and seated for her *riyaz*, plucking gently at the tanpura strings as she practised every note till it rang clear and true. Her long hair would be caught back in a loose knot, her face pure and innocent as she closed her eyes to draw out the *aaroha* of Raga Bhairav, an invocation to the sun. A gentle *karaman*, the morning breeze of Mandu, would blow in at the window and bring a smile to her face.

Baz stood at the bottom of the steps of Jahaz Mahal and felt the breeze on his face too, like a messenger willing him to turn in his path and walk to the Shahi Mahal. He shook his head and put his closed fist to his heart.

I shall not visit you, Roopmati, until I have controlled this great and consuming desire for you. Before it destroys me, and you, let us be apart. I am a man of my word, but I fear that I shall soon run out of words and take to action ...

Chapter 21

Roopmati waited impatiently for Sadiya to leave her alone. Her head ached; everything felt so wrong in her day, in her life. She missed her father terribly; she had not sung or played or composed for days now; and the worst, she had not seen the Sultan for over a week. It seemed that with every day that passed without a glimpse of Baz Bahadur, her spirits sank lower.

After that evening they had spent reading poetry to each other, he seemed to have disappeared from her life. Had she done something wrong? Had she spoken out of turn? Was there something that had angered him? She felt her temples start to throb again and turned to Sadiya, cutting her off in mid sentence. Of late, it also seemed that Sadiya spoke too much; there was no particular topic, she just carried on and on as if to fill that vacant look in Roopmati's eyes that twisted her own insides with sadness.

'Sadiya, my head aches! Can you bring me some soothing balm to apply on my brow please?'

Sadiya stared at Roopmati's face, her huge eyes bulging with concern.

'Ahhh! You are unwell, and I have been talking unceasingly of cockfights and fencing duels that must surely have made your pain increase! Forgive me, Bibijaan! I entreat you to lie down now. I will shade your room and spray sandal water, then make you a paste of herbs to apply on your brow!' She left the room calling out to Panna to bring herbs to her cooking quarters.

Nearly an hour later Roopmati lay in a darkened room with a soothing poultice on her brow. She must have drifted off, because waking, she suddenly became aware of a deep silence in the house and in the gardens around. There was the occasional call of a bird outside the window and the sound of her own breathing; little else. She lay still, savouring the quiet and the lightness of her head with the pain gone. She smiled. That silly Sadiya! Chattering like a monkey! But her knowledge was so deep and so wide that Roopmati would surely have loved to listen to her and absorb information on so many subjects from her. If only her heart did not ache like this she would not crave solitude to curl up into a tight ball and try and forget the Sultan ....

Solitude had been so elusive, these past few days. First it was the Sultana Hiba and her mother who had sent word with Panna, requesting an audience with her. She had acquiesced, wondering what the two women could want with her again.

~

They had come in their big palki, all smiles, and sat in the grand hall waiting for Sadiya to finish serving them sweetmeats, nuts and juices.

Finally alone with Roopmati, Jana Begum began.

'Ah dear Roopmati! It is indeed so heartening to see you in a better state than when we met last. It is obvious that the Sultan, my good son-in-law, is taking care of you!'

Roopmati nodded cautiously. The older woman continued, speaking with uncharacteristic effusiveness.

'Oh he is a good man, my son-in-law! Always ready to help his subjects, no matter who they are. And they in turn are deeply grateful, of course, but also get dejected. Do you know why? Because they are unable to ever repay him for his generous help in money, lands or goods.'

Roopmati nodded again, relieved that Jana Begum had summed up her very feelings.

'Yes, Begum Sahiba, I too feel the same. How can I ever repay the Sultan for all his help and support?'

Jana Begum laughed, a low, hacking laugh redolent of smug victory.

'Ah, Roopmati, there is always a way. I can suggest a way to return the Sultan's favours, but you may not feel it is appropriate.'

'Please tell me! I am eager to comply, no matter what your suggestion might be.'

'Well, there is a tradition here in Mandu that artistes of the court have their portraits painted and presented to the Sultan as a gift. Baz Bahadur values these as pieces of art and preserves them in his museum for posterity. Our court painter is very accomplished, and a respected man. I do not think you will have any complaints were he to paint your portrait. If you give permission, he could come here every day for perhaps a week to paint while you sit for him.'

Roopmati had begun shaking her head even before Jana Begum had finished speaking. Hiba shot a quick glance at her mother and pursed her lips.

'Have my portrait done! Oh no, no!' Roopmati laughed in disbelief.

Jana leaned forward and lowered her voice.

'I know what you are feeling. I too, when I was young, had my portrait made at my father's behest, but was too shy to sit face to face with the painter, an unknown man. Finally, I sat with my veil over my face and till today, they say, no one knows if it was really I who sat or was it some maidservant of mine!' She laughed her deep rumble and added, 'But those who know me well say my hands gave me away ... they were *such* pretty hands, you know.' Roopmati tried not to look at them directly.

Hiba shifted uneasily at the story and gave her mother another pointed look. Jana continued smoothly.

'Anyway, I just want to say that I understand how you feel, but in royal households, these feelings are not given any attention. A portrait is not just a painted picture, you know. It symbolises much more. As a gift, it shows respect for the receiver. It shows acknowledgement of his fine tastes. It means ...'

'But,' Roopmati broke in gently. 'I could perhaps think of some other gift to show the Sultan my gratitude ...'

'Some other gift for a man who has everything?' Jana Begum's smile was more of a sneer. 'My dear, what would you give him? A box of quills? Strings for his *been sitar*? A poem?'

Roopmati sat quietly, studying her hands.

'Roopmati, you are like my daughter. I want you to feel comfortable in our city. I want you to feel at home, not anxious that you may be a burden on the Sultan, living in this luxurious palace, being served by his servants and walking in his gardens every day. If it makes you feel more easy by presenting him some small gift, so be it. That is why I suggested a portrait of yourself to adorn his gallery of guests.'

'If you think he would like that ... '

'Of course he would. That is exactly what he would like, my dear. As I said, he is a connoisseur of the arts and the portrait would be a valuable addition to his art gallery.'

'And the painter ...'

'Rest your mind. He is a kindly old man, like a father to you.'

At the thought of her own father, Roopmati's eyes misted over and she nodded her head.

'I will do it.'

Later, Sadiya had glared at her in disbelief.

'Bibijaan, why did you agree to do what that old witch asked?'

Roopmati shook her head tiredly.

'We have been over it, Sadiya. She means well. I need to show my gratitude to the Sultan and this is what he will genuinely appreciate.'

'Who says so?'

'Please, Sadiya, let us not argue. Let me just get it over with. We will start tomorrow morning.'

Now lying in bed, her headache gone, Roopmati thought about the last week.

Well, it was not a very comfortable feeling, sitting for a portrait, but anything to repay the Sultan's hospitality. I must say the portrait was well made, and has been taken by Panna, all wrapped up, to Baz Bahadur's palace this morning. It will be presented as a gift from Roopmati. I do hope he likes it.

The late afternoon birdcalls continued. The monsoon was almost completely over and the evenings in Mandu seemed as if caught with a reed fan in one hand and one foot burrowing into a quilt. Did Baz Bahadur need a woman's body to keep him warm every night? She felt an unaccustomed jab deep in her stomach at the thought.

'Roopmati ...'

She lay still, with her eyes still closed. Her mind was playing tricks on her, of course.

'Are you feeling better now?'

She slowly opened her eyes and saw his shadowy figure in the dimness of the room. She felt a trembling happiness climb up from her chest and get caught in her throat. Tears pricked her eyes and she wanted to roll over and bury her face in the pillow and cry uncontrollably. The effect of suddenly facing him was overwhelming her.

He came close to the bed and knelt beside it. 'Roopmati, I ...' his voice was gruff and unsteady. 'Roopmati, I have to confess something to you. I have deliberately stayed away from you this past week.'

He waited for her to say something, but she couldn't. She just lay there looking up at him.

'I avoided you, because I wanted to believe my feelings for you were only empty attraction. I wanted to believe that I found you beautiful and desirable, that I was attracted to your voice, your music, and nothing more. I wanted to convince myself that if I stopped meeting you for some time, perhaps even go to other women,' there was a pause, then he continued softly, 'but I did not, I promise you. I wanted to believe that if I stopped meeting you for some time, I would stop wanting you so badly, day and night. Do you know what my promises mean, Roopmati? They are irrevocable. Once I give my word, I never go back. And I vowed to myself that I would keep my word to you and to your late father, that you would be here in Mandu as my singer and singing partner, nothing more.'

'But,' he continued, 'I was wrong. Not meeting you for seven days has driven me insane. I can think of nothing else but you! I have come to ask your forgiveness for staying away from you and the evening *mehfils* for so long! To also tell you that I plan to go away tomorrow on a trip to forge alliances with neighbouring states, then I may continue on a hunting trip. I may be away for weeks this time. Perhaps it would be best for both of us. There is a little gift for you I am leaving behind.' He got up lightly and fingertips touching his chin, turned to go.

Only half aware of her own actions, she tumbled out of the bed and reached him near the door. She slid her arms around him from the back and whispered into his broad muscular back, 'Do your promises to yourself mean the same if I break them?'

He turned slowly, disengaging her arms. For the first time, she looked into his eyes so close to her face, then closed her own as she felt his mouth prising open her lips and his trimmed beard rough on her cheek. She was giddy with the onslaught on her senses and melted into warm clay in his arms.

He undressed her and made love to her slowly, holding himself back, aware that it was her first time. As the room darkened into late evening, they became one in a long, gasping union that was beyond anything Baz had ever experienced and Roopmati could ever have imagined. Then they lay together, Roopmati trailing her fingers over his bare chest. She felt there was nothing more she could ever ask for in her life, again. Everything was perfect.

They slept, bodies entangled, and waking often to touch and caress and arouse each other again, and again. The drapes at the window had turned pale by the time Baz reluctantly lifted his face buried in her silken shoulder.

'I have to go. I have some things to attend to in court today. Then I will cancel my trip and come back to you in the evening again. Goodbye, my beautiful nymph.'

At the door he turned and said, 'See my gift and tell me later if you like it.'

She raised herself on an elbow and said, 'Oh, I cannot wait to see it! And,' she asked teasingly, 'how did you like my gift? Has it reached you yet?'

Baz turned as he was fastening his jacket.

'What gift?' He looked mystified.

'Oh oh, I should not have mentioned it!' She covered her face.

'No. Tell me.' He came up to her, fully dressed.

'The portrait, of course.'

He froze. 'Portrait?'

'Yes, the one of me done by the court painter. To be sent to you.'

She saw his expression harden in the early morning light.

'No portrait of you was sent to me. Who sent a painter to you? Who asked for the portrait?'

'Hiba Begum's mother Jana Begum.'

Baz slapped his brow and placing his hands on his hips looked up at the ceiling, fighting to stay calm.

''Please tell me you are not serious. That this is some kind of a joke, but if it is, it's in poor taste.'

Roopmati fell silent, studying his face.

'Why are you so upset? I don't understand.'

His eyes were blazing.

'Really? You don't understand? I have kept you from all male eyes until now, and now you let a ... a *painter* sit here day after day, staring at you, sizing up your ... your assets, painting your body, your hair ... your skin! Really? You don't understand?'

'You ... did not want that?'

'When did I ever ask for it?'

'She ... I'm sorry ... Jana Begum said you did. That it was a court tradition to have the portrait done of every artiste and presented to the Sultan.'

Baz slapped his brow again and she gazed at his face uneasily, wondering how he could have been transformed from a passionate lover into this incensed stranger within minutes.

'I ...' she began.

'Silence!' He whirled around, almost beside himself with rage. 'You don't know anything! These people are playing a game with you! They are trying to get rid of you, don't you see? There is no portrait, Roopmati! There is only a plan and a plot and players and pawns here!'

'But there *is* a portrait! I have seen it!'

'Ahh! A portrait of the very beautiful Roopmati! Of course!' he sneered. 'And where is that portrait? Which man's hands has it fallen into? Do you even care?'

She looked at him silently, tears pricking her eyes.

'Roopmati's picture can fall into any hands, but does it matter to her? Oh no, no, no! Because she doesn't care! If not Baz, then any man can gaze at her, any man can even woo her! She doesn't care!' He brought a fist up to his chest and looking straight at her, prodded it twice with his thumb. Then he was gone.

Chapter 22

The rider slowed down and brought his horse to a standstill as Agra Fort loomed on the horizon, an emperor in its own right over the plebeian vista of low houses and hutments cluttered around it. Its towering red brick walls though worn by war and torn by strife stood yet an awe-inspiring symbol of Mughal might and power, a statement of invincibility. The man had been riding all night with the large, window-sized package securely fastened behind him with strict instructions from the Begum.

'The parcel should not get damaged nor wet nor fall from the horse. It is a very valuable piece of art that I am sending to the Mughal Emperor's court. Take it straight to my nephew, Adham Khan, commander of the Emperor's forces and hand it over to him with my compliments. My detailed message is in this sealed letter. Now go, and do not stop on the way unless waylaid by robbers or killed by lightning!'

Now the messenger skirted the towering inward-tilted defences of the fort to reach the Akbari Darwaza on the south-western turn of the wall. He waited for the bridge to be lowered over the moat, then identified himself to the guards and cantered in. He was relieved; his mission was almost done and he could hand over the parcel and go to the military barracks to eat, drink and sleep. Jana Begum was a hard taskmaster, but the rewards she handed out were well worth all the trouble. A bag of copper coins jingled in his pocket. There would be another to collect once he returned with a reply from Adham Khan.

Accompanied by an armed horseman of the fort's security guards, he made his way past the Diwan-e-Aam, hall of public audience and the *baoli,* the step well that had been created in Babur's time, towards the living quarters of the nobles and courtiers. Adham Khan lived in a mahal which had its own section to house his wife and her retinue of servants. His mother Maham Anga, however, preferred to live with the other women in the zenana.

The messenger was searched at the entrance before being let in through several sets of double doors until he finally found himself in a longish room, thickly carpeted and covered with bows and muskets and spears over every wall. It was an aggressively masculine room and smelt faintly of sweat and leather. Adham Khan was by the window, examining the sharpness of a spear's blade. He turned at the announcement and studied the messenger waiting with the wrapped parcel in his arms. Finally he spoke, roughly.

'What is your mission?'

The man bowed low and said, 'Huzoor, I bring you a gift and a letter from Jana Begum Sahiba, mother-in-law of the Sultan of Malwa and your own maternal aunt.'

'Hmm. Leave both here. You may go.'

'I have been asked to bring a reply, Huzoor.'

Adham Khan sneered. 'You will be advised of that before you leave the fort. Now go!'

When the door had closed behind the messenger and his escort, Adham looked thoughtfully at the large package. What could Khalajaan have sent him all the way from Malwa? Her last suggestion to him had ended badly with his overtures to Baz Bahadur being summarily rejected. Could this be some kind of peace offering, or was there a deeper plot afoot? Adham smiled. His Khalajaan was no simpleton; she was a master strategist and had displayed her skills several times, not least of them in getting her daughter married to Baz Bahadur, eldest son of the late Sultan, and heir to the lion's share of the kingdom on his father's passing.

This must be something very significant. Adham picked up the parcel and slit the strings and wrappings with his spear. Then he held up the painting to the light and stood, astounded.

The woman in the painting was exquisite, her features perfectly proportioned, eyes large and dreamy, hair and skin glowing in a soft light. Adham felt his heart leap in his chest. Could this be the same woman whose singing talents Khalajaan had extolled in her last letter? Impossible; no woman could be both so beautiful and so talented.

He placed the painting on a chair, and still holding on to it with a hand, shook open the letter from his aunt.

My very dear nephew Adham, may Allah shower his choicest blessings upon you. I send here to you this gift of a painting. This is Roopmati, the singer of whom I had written to you last time. It is a great tragedy that your proposition to bring her to Emperor Akbar's court in exchange for the hand of Mughal friendship and support was rejected summarily by the Sultan, my son-in-law. That is why I have been forced to take further action. You see, dear Adham, the need to move Roopmati from Mandu to Agra is more than just an official diplomatic gesture. It is a necessity to save the relationship of my poor daughter, your sister Hiba, with Baz. My son-in-law is besotted with Roopmati ... Ah! what bitterness those words flood into my heart and before he falls completely into her spell to the extent of forgetting both his family duties and his kingdom, I wish to remove this scourge from the bounds of Malwa.

I trust that a single glimpse of this beauty would have convinced you of the need to bring her to your own mahal for your sole pleasure. I entreat you to appeal to the Emperor to allow you to make an advance on Malwa and do hereby assure you that your prize shall be nothing less than Roopmati.

My warm regards to your mother, my dear sister.

I await your early response, your affectionate Khalajaan.

Adham Khan held up the painting again and gazed in silence at the doe-like eyes, the full lips, the long neck and the curves below. He felt a stirring in his loins.

Yes, I must possess this woman. I will do as Khalajaan suggests and take my forces out and bring back my own spoils of battle to enjoy at leisure ... Roopmati.

Emperor Akbar sat on his gilded throne carved with tiger's heads on the back and arms and surveyed the faces of his council of ministers. Closest to his throne sat his *ichkis*, his closest advisors, Bairam Khan, Ahmad Khan, Ataga Khan and Adham Khan. The wooden pavilion they were all seated in was of an awkward shape, mainly octagonal, but widening and deepening on one of the sides to accommodate the Emperor's throne and the *jali* screens at the sides and back, behind which sat the women in power ... his queens and his mother and his paternal aunt. The pavilion, perched on a wind-swept terrace overlooking the Yamuna, acted as the official meeting chamber for Akbar and his ministers, though it had obviously been designed long ago for other uses.

Akbar looked around at the weather beaten wood panels, mouldings and carvings and to his heightened aesthetic senses, they felt like a thorn in the flesh, making him wince every time his eyes took in the sight.

This is supposed to be my very exclusive private audience chamber, my diwan-e-khas. And yet, it is like the recreation room of my bodyguard! When my father and I seized Hindustan back from Sher Shah Suri, and came back to our capital Agra and rode into this fort, what a decrepit state it was in! But not for long. I shall build up the fort into a new glory, fully fit for the Emperor of the world to live in with his queens and concubines and sons and commanders. But it is also true that in spite of its warts and scars, this fort still remains the most awe-inspiring symbol of the conquest of Hindustan.

The ministers and nobles of the court were waiting for him to speak.

'I have called this meeting today,' began Akbar, 'to felicitate each one of you on the Mughal Empire of which we have jointly laid the foundation. Having vanquished Adil Shah's *sipahsalar* Hemu and his forces in Panipat and taken our territories back from him, we have achieved a major victory for the Mughals which my father Humayun, and indeed my grandfather Babur would have been greatly proud of. But,' he held up a hand as the courtiers began to murmur their praises, 'but we have only laid the foundation as I said. There is a long, long way to go and many, many campaigns to fight and victories to gain before we can say that our empire has touched the four corners of the earth!'

He looked around at his coterie of loyal advisors, his commanders and his milk brother, Adham Khan. He sensed the approval of his mother Hamida and aunt Gulbadan behind the latticed wooden screen.

'I have called this meeting today to discuss with you all our future campaigns. There are the Rajputana states to subjugate, starting from the Mewar state of Chittorgarh, whose arrogant Rana Udai Singh needs to be defeated, then Gujarat that is already weak with political turmoil where the ruler Ahmad Shah is controlled by his nobles. Then there is Malwa, with its capital at Mandavgarh, and Gondwana beyond that. There is the Deccan to invade in the South, Bengal in the east and Sind and Kashmir in the North. We must plan our campaigns carefully, keeping in mind who our greatest enemies or threats are.'

There was general assent and the nobles began to stand up one by one, holding forth on the subject, each giving his point of view. Akbar listened carefully, mentally making notes to himself on which opinions were worth considering. At a pause in the dialogues, Adham Khan stood up, exuding arrogance and looked around. Then he turned to the emperor and spoke.

'Jahanpanah, I believe that there is another way to plan our campaigns. Not just with the consideration of which kingdoms or states are our biggest threats, but also which is our path to these kingdoms!'

Akbar raised his eyebrows.

'Kindly explain yourself, Adham Khan.'

Adham indicated to a minion who ran up with a rolled canvas. He unfurled it and held it up for the court to see. There was a map of Hindustan drawn on it.

'Here is Gujarat and here is Rajputana, Malwa, Gondwana...' Adham pointed with a slim velvet-tipped rod. 'So, if you are planning to capture Gujarat, you should ideally subjugate Rajputana first and it will cut a natural path southwards to Gujarat for you. Or, you could choose a weaker state, such as Malwa to beat an easy route to Gondwana, which is presently ruled by the fearless Rani Durgavati on behalf of her minor son. Or again, you could defeat the forces of Malwa's Sultan to reach Gujarat to its west.'

There was a short silence. Then Akbar nodded his head slowly.

'You have a point, Adham. Your thinking is good. We need to plan our campaigns on these lines.'

Flushed with success and inner excitement, Adham continued speaking.

'Jahanpanah, I propose that we immediately prepare our armies to leave for the Malwa plains, where we will attack the Sultan Baz Bahadur's army ... a weak and poorly prepared one I am glad to report, and having done that, proceed upwards to the Mandu fort, where the treasury can be ransacked, their monuments torn down and their water bodies poisoned for posterity.'

Akbar raised his hand and made his pronouncement.

'We shall take Malwa first, then proceed to Gondwana. It is a powerful province and will indeed be a jewel in our crown.' He looked straight at Adham Khan. 'Even in war, we must maintain our humanity and our principles. No harm should be brought to the ancient fort of Mandu, nor to their women and children. Take their soldiers prisoners and carry away the valuables from their treasury, but spare everything else.' He looked around. 'The war council will meet tomorrow morning at eight.'

Akbar walked out, followed by his entourage. Adham watched him go, a small, inscrutable smile on his face.

Chapter 23

'Bibijaan, wake up! The sun is high above our heads!'

The voice seemed to come out of a deep well. Roopmati opened eyes heavy with sleep and raised her face from the pillow into which she had buried it, just minutes back, it seemed.

She had watched the door close behind Baz and then thrown herself face down on the bed, her mouth trembling at his rebuff so soon after they had spent the night together in deep intimacy.

Bewildered by his anger, she had pulled a pillow to her and buried her face in it, inhaling his smell that lingered there. Then everything went a velvety black as she sank into a deep, deep sleep, the body exhausted from the lovemaking and the mind from the confrontation they had just had.

At Sadiya's persistent calls, she dragged herself out of bed, then glancing down at herself, hastily wound her sari around her body and opened the door.

'Oh Bibijaan! I am sorry to wake you, but it is so late, and I was anxious about you!' She looked beyond at the rumpled bed and lowered one eyelid playfully. 'So, Sultan has gone, I see!'

'You knew he was here?' Roopmati couldn't meet her eyes.

'Of course, I know everything that happens in your life, Bibijaan! I was awake when he came in last evening. In fact, it was I who told him that you were unwell; showed him into your room. When he left this morning, I must have fallen asleep in the hall. If I had known you're alone, I would have come to check on you earlier.'

'Thank you, Sadiya. Oh, I have slept too much! I will quickly take a bath and get ready. Can you bring a pot of hot water to the bathroom immediately?'

'Yes Bibijaan, water is heated and ready in the kitchen, I will bring it.'

In the bathroom, Roopmati undressed and looked down at herself; her body looked different, more full and ripe and with purpling patches ... somehow, like a bruised fruit that had fallen from the tree. Too shy to let Sadiya see her like this, she locked the door and bathed, her mind dwelling on what had happened the previous night, but refusing to think of what had ensued early this morning.

'Will you be going to the pavilion today to see the Narmada, Bibijaan?' asked Sadiya, chattering away on trivial matters, as she combed her mistress's long hair in front of the wall mirror. Her eyes quietly studied Roopmati's face in the reflection, trying to gauge her state of mind.

'Yes, ummm ... no.' Roopmati was in no mood to do anything. She was wondering if the Sultan had finished dealing with his court matters and left on his long trip. She felt a sense of hollowness inside at the thought, as if there was nothing within her anymore if he was not around.

'Bibijaan, is everything all right?' Roopmati caught Sadiya's anxious expression in the mirror and suddenly felt a strong need to confide in her.

She shook her head and caught her lip between her teeth.

'Tell me.'

Sadiya came and sat on the floor at Roopmati's feet, her eyes trusting and trustworthy. Roopmati nodded and slowly, disjointedly, poured out the story about the portrait and how she had asked the Sultan if he had liked her gift, and then what had happened after that.

'Gift! Oh Bibijaan, I forgot! The Sultan's gift to you is kept with me, he had left it in the entrance hall and I kept it safe.'

'No, no! I don't want to see it yet, Sadiya! He has always been so good to me ... so very generous ... and I ... I ... You don't understand, Sadiya! The Sultan thinks I am cheap and promiscuous to have posed for the painter! I am overcome with shame at the memory of the words he said to me!'

Sadiya shook her large head.

'No, no, Bibijaan, you have misunderstood the Sultan's feelings! He loves you so much that he is possessive, that's why he was so angry, he wanted to hurt you. But you know something, Bibijaan? He has hurt himself the most!'

'How?'

'Did you know that the Sultan was supposed to attend to some court matters today and then leave for a trip?'

Roopmati nodded.

'Well, he has not done either!' Sadiya's expression was triumphant.

Roopmati worried her lower lip, unsure whether to be thrilled that he was still in Mandu, or to be concerned that he was not attending to his duties.

'Bibijaan, the Sultan is an emotional man, a man of poetry and music and art! And he is now deeply in love with you, and distressed that another man laid eyes on you for days as he painted. How can he attend to his royal duties when he has quarrelled with you?'

Roopmati flushed and looked down at her hands. Sadiya quickly got up and bustled out of the room, muttering something. She was back in a few minutes, carrying a large soft parcel, her face almost hidden behind it.

'His gift to you.'

She beamed as Roopmati opened it. A dress slid out, wrapped in unbleached muslin. Roopmati shook it out, then gasped. It was a lehenga and choli in pure white cotton, embellished with tiny silver and gold *buttis* all over the skirt. The choli and dupatta were edged with delicate gold and silver zari, but beyond that, there was no other work on them.

Roopmati gazed at the pristine fine cotton billowing like foam. He had remembered that she only wore cotton and never any heavily embellished clothes, so he had got this dress specially made for her. It was his subtle request to her to wear the lehenga-choli of his culture just once to please him.

She lifted it to her face and rubbed the softness dreamily on her cheek.

'So, Bibijaan? Will you wear it tonight?'

'Tonight? What is tonight?' Roopmati was taken aback.

Sadiya smiled with the wisdom of the ages.

'Tonight, Bibijaan, I will send you to the Sultan's palace, dressed in this. You will go to meet him like his bride, his queen, his consort.'

The moon was rising between the trees, its silver-gold glow half hidden by the feathery fronds of ferns.

Roopmati glanced out of the window as Sadiya pinned tiny gold and silver stars on the top of her dark head, from where her tresses cascaded down to her waist.

'Sadiya, the moon looks big today, does it not?'

'Bibijaan, it is the twelfth day of the growing moon today. Just a few days more to the full moon.'

'Hmmm. Sadiya, are you sure the Sultan will be in his palace tonight?'

'Bibijaan, where will he go when he is yearning for you?'

'He can come here to me if what you say is true!' Roopmati's reply was spirited and faintly indignant.

'He is a hot tempered man, Bibijaan. His anger does not cool quickly, that's why he is very passionate in love!'

Roopmati's breath caught as she remembered. She quickly stood up and turned to her companion.

"How do I look, Sadiya?'

Sadiya studied her with eyes shining with fond indulgence and nodded silently. They walked out together to where Panna stood talking to the two palki bearers waiting near the covered carriage. As she sat down in the palki with Sadiya by her side,

Roopmati sensed rather than saw Panna's resentful glare in the moonlight. The bearers picked up the palki and they set off.

The lights, the music, the voices from the Jahaz Mahal, the Tabeli Mahal and the hamamghar complexes began to die away as the palki swayed south, towards the Sultan's complex, and Roopmati began to glimpse another Mandu by night. The path wound between dark forests from which a pack of golden jackals, just dark shadows now, began to bay and howl setting off raucous shrieks of langurs from the treetops. The lakes shimmered silently in the moonlight and the silhouettes of monuments in the distance looked like ghostly remains of another age. Roopmati looked up at the sky and spoke softly,

Tonight I go to greet the moon
And welcome her new shining face
Ah! Double joy! Thy eyes and mine
Fixed on one place

The palki took the final turn in the path and skirted the Rewa Kund as it approached Baz Bahadur's palace. When the bearers set the carriage down carefully, Roopmati alighted and first turned to pay her respects to the Rewa Kund.

Ma Narmada, be with me in this difficult moment as I seek him who I love the most in this world ...

Then she spoke softly to Sadiya.

'Please wait here. I will be back soon.'

She looked up at the palace and it struck her that it looked dark as if the lamps within had not been lit. Her doubts rushed back. Had the Sultan gone to Jahaz Mahal, to his concubines? Or had he sought his wife Hiba's arms again? She almost turned back, but the sudden image of Sadiya sending her like a proud mother would a beloved daughter to her son-in-law's house made her pause, and lifting the hem of her skirt she began to climb the steps. No matter what, she, Roopmati, would make the first move to placate Baz Bahadur. Because there was no place for pride in true love.

The two guards outside the palace raised their swords, then recognising her, lowered them and let her through. The steps were shallow and broad; Roopmati had barely noticed them the last time she had come here. She walked along a covered corridor dimly lit with sconces along the walls. The passage turned right and opened into a courtyard on one side. As she hesitated below its arched entrance, a small, stooped figure stepped out of the shadows, perhaps a manservant, and bending his head respectfully, waved a hand to another arch. She entered another passage that twisted and turned artfully. Just as Roopmati began to worry about where this passage was leading her she found herself in a large, moonlit courtyard. She stood stock still, her breath snatched away by the beauty of the scene. The moon had disappeared behind clouds, but still radiated a magical luminosity to the world. All along the walls of the courtyard were life-sized statues of men and women in various poses, sculpted in red granite. They glowed a pale pink in the dim light. In the centre of the courtyard, almost covering its length and breadth, was a large pool with steps leading down into the water from all sides. The water, dark and mysterious, rippled and splashed gently in the breeze.

And then she saw him.

Baz Bahadur was in the pool, lying back in his favourite pose, arms stretched along the ledge and legs splayed out to keep afloat. He seemed to be lost in his thoughts.

Roopmati stood as still as one of the statues, suddenly wishing she could leave surreptitiously without him sighting her.

Baz lay back and looked up at the sky. The clouds were scudding in from the East, bringing a cool breeze with them. Soon, the cold weather would be upon them.

His thoughts were desultory, but his feelings were intense, restless. All he wanted was to be with Roopmati in the Shahi Mahal, wrapped in her arms, whispering endearments into her shell-like ear and waking up every morning to the beauty of her body and heart. And yet, he had spoken harshly to her this very morning and did not have the courage to face her now. Perhaps, in a few days, she would forgive him and send a message and ...

Just then, his eyes fell on a figure standing near the arched entrance of the courtyard. There had never been a statue there. He came upright and looked again. Had the figure moved? At that moment, the moon came out from behind a cloud.

Is this an illusion? Is it my longing coming to life? It cannot be ...

He stared unbelievingly at Roopmati standing there, radiant in the white lehenga set he had got made especially for her. She looked back at him silently, making no attempt to hide her trembling lip and unshed tears from his gaze.

Then, as if there had been unspoken words between them, she began to walk slowly to the edge of the pool. Her eyes still locked with his, she descended the steps, the cotton lehenga soaking and beginning to wrap itself around her body. She came down and stood chest deep in the water and waited.

Baz began to walk towards her, his hands pushing the water back. He stopped in front of her. They were both breathing hard, as if they had been swimming and had just come up for air.

'Meri jal pari,' he whispered.

He reached out and pulled at the strings of her choli and peeled it slowly away, down her arms, just as he had in his dreams. He let it float, then untied her lehenga and lifted it, wet and unwieldy, over her head. Finally, left clad in only a string of pearls around her neck and on her wrist, she wrapped her arms over her breasts and shivered, not with the cold, but with rising excitement. He gently pulled her arms away.

'You have nothing to hide from me, Roopmati,' he said. She closed her eyes as she felt his strong, muscular arms around her, his urgent lips devouring hers. With soft moans and gasps, they strained to fuse their bodies together, to become one. As she drowned in the pool of sensations, Roopmati knew nothing else mattered any more.

Roopmati did not leave the palace for three days.

They remained confined to Baz's large and richly furnished chamber, curtains drawn against the light, never knowing when it was day and when night.

Once, she struggled to break free of his arms on a sudden thought.

'Sadiya! I told her to wait. She must be there still!'

He laughed and pulled her down onto the pillow.

'No, my beautiful, caring woman. She and the palki bearers were sent away that very night by my manservant.'

'How? How did ...'

Baz laughed again.

'My staff is clever enough to know who their Sultan was longing for and that when she arrived, he would never let her go ...'

He ran his finger over her stomach.

'Are you hungry now?'

She nodded.

He rang a bell by the door. After 10 minutes, a discreet cough told them their tray of food had been left outside. Baz waited, then went to bring it in.

Later, as she lay on her side, propped by an elbow, curling a strand of hair between her fingers, he whispered., 'You make a beautiful picture, do you know?'

She whispered back, 'Only for you.' He understood the meaning in her words, the contrition in her tone. He nodded and traced a finger over her curves.

'I will be the only artist to draw you.'

He bent and ran his tongue down her neck and over her shoulder. 'And to paint you.'

They lay together, heads on the pillow, and talked for hours. Of his childhood and his brothers and their pranks and of her carefree youth on the banks of the river, shepherding cattle and playing games. He didn't speak of his enmity with Daulat and Mustafa in recent years, how there had been bloodshed and killing; he didn't want to spoil the mood. There would be time later to tell her everything in his heart.

They made love again and again, as if life was short and they had to make the most of these precious hours together. When he lay with his head on her lap, there was no more need to say anything, do anything. They were at peace, just together.

Several times, there was the sound of boots in the courtyard and a voice asking permission to speak. But Baz ignored it and the footsteps receded.

'What could they want of you? Do you think there is something important that needs your attention?' she asked anxiously.

'Nothing is more important than this,' he said and began to caress her again.

~

A set of her clothes had arrived from Shahi Mahal, sent by the ever thoughtful Sadiya. On the fourth day, she began to prepare to leave.

As she stood fully dressed, brushing her hair in front of the mirror and studying her glowing eyes shadowed by nights without sleep, he came up behind and encircled her slim waist.

'Don't go,' he said into her neck. 'Let us live like this forever.'

'Baz!' She turned around.

'Ah, how good my name sounds on your tongue!'

'Baz, I am aware that there are matters of the court, and concerns with your provinces and nearby territories that you have not given any attention to in the last few days. I need to leave, so that you can start working.'

He nodded reluctantly. 'Yes. But I will look into everything as quickly as possible and come to you again.'

'Promise?'

'I promise.'

He touched his fist to his heart in his own style and she laughed in sheer joy.

Chapter 24

There were more military, political and internal matters demanding his attention than Baz had expected. Due to a heavy monsoon, some of the crops had been destroyed in the plains and they would need to procure more wheat and millet in exchange for their cash crops like cotton and flax. Which meant that there would be less flow into the exchequer this year. Then the farmers and labourers would have to be compensated from the royal treasury and their houses rebuilt for them.

The military was generally in poor shape and low in morale, the commander explained to the Sultan in a private audience with him. The troops needed more weaponry and food supplies and funds for training, and they were badly in need of hundreds more of horses and at least one more fleet of war elephants. An epidemic in the stables had cut down the numbers of war animals dangerously.

For two days now, Baz had sat through hour after hour, session after session of discussions with his ministers and commanders. But his mind was never fully with any of them. His yearning for Roopmati was like a voice in his head that drowned out every other voice.

She had become an opiate in his veins, creating heightened sensations in his brain and a feeling of euphoria when with her, but when away from her, plunging him into a state of craving and misery.

Is this love, or is it just obsession? He asked himself even as the agriculture minister read out pages of statistics to him.

I can't think of anything else but Roopmati, am I going out of my mind? He agonised as the army commander gave him an account of food supplies and ammunition that were needed.

I am only half alive in her absence ... does that mean I am half dead? He wondered with a self-deprecating smile as the home minister explained the extent of rain-related damage incurred all over the kingdom.

All this budgeting and administration and diplomacy and military strategy, it is beyond the boundaries of my interest! All I want is my Roopmati and my music and the peace of Mandu to enjoy them both in! Is that too much to ask?

Sitting on his ornate chair in Hindola Mahal, hearing all the grievances and proposals from his advisors, Baz suddenly straightened up and looked around.

'Do whatever you all think is good for our kingdom of Malwa. There is nothing I can add to whatever you have already suggested. Royal Treasurer Naseer Khan, here are the keys to the strong room. Distribute the funds as required to each minister.'

'But, Huzoor, the treasury is depleted. We have been dipping into it for the last two years, with barely anything going back in.'

'Hmmm. What about the taxes you have collected from our farmers and landowners?'

'The farmers are starving and have barely enough to feed themselves. The taxes we collect from the landowners and merchants do not even cover the needs of the army which is in dire need of ...'

Baz held up an authoritative hand.

'Yes, yes, I know! I have already heard about what the Army needs!'

The Army commander stepped forward.

'Huzoor, our kingdom is only as secure as our army is well-organised. Even the slightest threat from other states can endanger us if our soldiers and war animals are not well equipped to fight.'

Baz was angry. He looked around, his eyes blazing.

'Enough! I will not hear another word from any of you! I have already said that the Treasury is open and the Treasurer may disburse funds to all as required! Now you may go.'

He got up and strode out, his personal bodyguard running behind him.

Roopmati was back in her favourite position by the window of the large hall, her fingers plucking at the strings of the tanpura. She drew out the opening notes of the *Yaman Kalyan*, then as her eyes drank in the beauty of a sunset sky drenched in colour, paused and smiled, lost in her thoughts.

Life was so beautiful, so perfect, that her heart ached with happiness. Baz was hers and only hers, of this the last few days had convinced her. He wanted to marry her, make her his principal queen, have fine sons and beautiful daughters with her, and spend all their days together, making love and making music.

She missed him, in fact, ever since they had parted two days ago, she had felt as if she had left half of herself behind in his palace. But it did not matter; Baz had to attend to his royal duties, ensure that his people were secure, well-fed, well-administered. Perhaps he would need to make a diplomatic visit to nearby ally states too. She had no idea how much time he would take to come back to her, but she would be patient. And when at last they met, their union would be all the sweeter for the time they had spent apart.

Her fingers stilled on the strings of the instrument and she softly spoke a few lines that she had penned the night before.

Hour after hour I turn and toss,
Sleep cometh not to me forlorn,
Lacking the opiate of thy kiss
At night, at morn.

Suddenly, the jingle of a horse's bridle, male voices, and booted feet on the steps outside broke her reverie. She knew those footsteps. Her heart thumping, she looked towards the door just as Baz came in, towering and regal in his court formals. Her insides turned to warm candle wax as she lay aside the tanpura and stood up. Within minutes, they were in her chamber, reaching for each other.

Later, as they lay together, Roopmati asked huskily, 'I thought you would take a few days, maybe even a few weeks to get the affairs of the state under control.'

'Yes, I thought so too.'

'But?'

'Well, let me just say that all this planning and budgeting and administration and rehabilitation is not exactly what I am cut out to do. I have told my ministers to take care of everything.'

There was a short silence, then Roopmati raised herself on an elbow and looked into Baz's face, so young and attractive, so relaxed with his eyes closed.

'Baz.'

'Hmm?'

'I think your presence is needed there in the court. They cannot take such big decisions on their own. They need your guidance, they need funds, they need ...'

Baz pulled her down, turned on his side and threw a leg over her body. He then traced a finger under her eyes.

'You seem like you have not slept for days, *jaanu*. What were you doing?'

She coloured and caught his wrist.

'Stop. Were you even listening to what I was saying?'

'Umm ... yes and no. I heard something about my presence being needed. Well, here I am. Now go to sleep and I will hold you in my arms all night.'

She sighed her acquiescence and snuggled down. Within minutes they were both blissfully asleep.

~

Hiba sighed deeply as she stood at her window and looked out at the front courtyard of her palace, aglow with lighted fountains and floating diyas dancing on the splash pools. She felt utterly lonely; there were longings in her heart she could not express, and a raw, burning need within her body that she could not contain. She was so ready for love, but there was no one to love. And so full of desires, but there was no one to satisfy them.

On a sudden whim, she whirled around and faced her maidservant. Nasi was quietly preparing her room for the night. She was alarmed when she saw the Sultana looking at her speculatively. Hiba's temper tantrums and penchant for throwing the nearest object at her hapless minions petrified Nasi.

'Nasi!' Hiba's voice sounded a trifle desperate, even to her own ears. 'Nasi, I am so bored! Take me somewhere, anywhere! Take me out where all of you go for entertainment. Where do you go? Where do your men folk go, every night? Tell me, tell me!'

'Oh Huzoor, you cannot possibly go where my brother and other men go in the nights! Those are not good places for you!'

Hiba frowned and made a dismissive sound.

'Pffft! I don't mean the whore houses, of course, you silly girl! I mean the places for wager sports and dancing and singing and drama! I have heard that those places are packed to the roof at night and full of noise and revelry ! Is it true?'

Nasi looked at the uncharacteristically vulnerable expression on the Sultana's face and nodded eagerly. Before she knew it, she was chattering breathlessly to her mistress.

'Yes, Huzoor! Many times when my duty here finishes, I go with other maids from the palaces with our brothers and cousins to these places and make small bets. But it is not the winning that we go for, but the *raunaq*, the crowds, the cheering and jeering that make our hearts to beat fast and our heads to throb! We love the feeling of being one with hundreds of others, screaming for our team to win! Believe me, Huzoor, it is more than an opium high!'

Hiba's eyes were shining.

'Ahh ... that is just what I need!' she exclaimed excitedly. 'A dose of opium that will not put me to sleep, but wake me up! I want to be out of this dreary palace ... out in the streets, in the fighting arenas, in the amphitheatres, watching, participating, experiencing life! Nasi,' she caught the girl by her shoulders and shook her gently. 'Nasi, you have to take me with you. Tonight!'

Nasi tried to wriggle out of the grip, a little scared by what she had unleashed.

'Oh Huzoor, you cannot come with us! What will your mother say? What will the Sultan do if he finds out?'

Hiba's lip curled in scorn.

'If he cared about me or my whereabouts, I would not be standing here by my window every night, alone and lonely. Let us go!' She reached for her silken veil.

Nasi stopped her.

'No, no, Huzoor, you cannot come out in your fine clothes! Give me a day and I will get some peasant clothes stitched for you. *Then* you will be ready to go out!'

The next night, Hiba stood before the full length mirror, dressed in a simple cotton ghagra and a thick black burkha to go over it. Not just the look, but even the very feel of her costume made her flinch in distaste.

'Let us remove your gold rings and bangles, Huzoor. They will give you away as being of noble blood.' Nasi painstakingly put away the jewellery and produced a pair of rough camel leather *joothis* for her feet. She studied Hiba proudly exclaiming, 'Ah! Now you will not stand out in our midst. We cannot have any one sighting the Sultana jostling among the masses and watching a blood sport with them!'

Hiba smiled in secret anticipation at the word blood sport, wondering at her own need for such a base level of entertainmemt. Ever since she had overheard two of the servant girls gossiping as they polished silver in a corner of the chamber her curiosity had been aroused.

One of the girls had declared, 'My husband goes cockfighting every night and comes back with empty pockets. I have told him time and again not to place any bets but go just to watch the fun.'

'Cockfighting! Oh I really enjoy that! My brother and I go to the rings whenever I get some time off from the Mahal. We have won so much, you know! 16 *pice* in three days!'

Watching the girls exclaiming and giggling, Hiba's curiosity had been aroused. She called them near.

'What is this cockfighting like? I have never seen a fight myself, though I am aware that it goes on in Mandu every night and attracts lots of people.'

'Oh, Begum Hiba! Cockfighting is so exciting, so fast and so furious! You see the two roosters, place your bets on one, then watch them attack each other, and the game is over before you know it!'

'You mean one of them dies?' Hiba's pulse thumped.

They both nodded excitedly. 'Yes, and it is carried off by the victor, the owner of the victorious cock, I mean, and cooked into a tasty meal!'

'And Huzoor, the *baazigar*s who bet on the winning cock get their share of the *raqam*! Oh, the excitement of winning night after night!'

The other one muttered, 'You wait, your luck too will run out and you will not be laughing so much then!'

Hiba threw back her curls with a sudden decision and rang the bell for Nasi. 'We will go and watch a cockfight tonight,' she said.

'But, Huzoor, cockfights are so violent! Are you sure you can take the noise and the smells and the bloodshed?'

For a fleeting moment, Hiba looked like her mother, all disdain and annoyance. 'I am a very strong person, you know! I will prove it to you in the cockfighting arena!'

Now that the hand-drawn cart Nasi had brought from their village was ready and the evening had settled in, the girls put on their burkhas, settled Hiba on the narrow wooden plank of the cart and set off. Hiba gritted her teeth against the rattles and jolts that shook her as they set off. At the entrance to the round, low-roofed building, a pimply young man came out of the crowds to meet them.

'My brother,' whispered one of the girls. 'We cannot go in without a man to accompany us.'

Hiba nodded, her heart thudding. Coming out in the night, mingling with the commoners doing something forbidden, was so exciting. When the big wooden gates opened, they merged with the crowds and were practically carried in on a wave of pushing, shoving humanity.

There was a huge circular fenced area inside the enclosure. The crowds milled around the fence.

'Oh!' Hiba turned to the youth and addressed him through the burkha. 'We forgot to place our bets!'

He turned to his sister, though how he knew her from the other girls through their masks was a mystery, and looked blank. She nodded her head reassuringly at Hiba.

'Oh my brother has already placed our bets. Tonight, Huzoor, you just watch and learn, all right?'

At that instant there was an ear-splitting blast from a trumpet. As two men entered the ring with a bird each in their hands, the crowds began to shout lustily. Hiba noticed that one rooster had a yellow band on its leg and the other, a blue one.

'What is that just above the band?' asked Hiba, 'It looks like another claw.'

'No, no, Huzoor, that is a *kanta,* a cockspur. It is made of sharpened tortoiseshell and tied to the cock's leg to make the game more interesting.'

There was a roar from the crowd as the birds were released. Immediately they began to attack each other. Their necks stretched long, their wings flapping furiously, they pecked and scratched and clawed. Hiba watched the gory scene through her netted eye-piece, her hands over her mouth. Feathers flew, the dust rose in clouds and still the roosters fought their bloody fight. Then she became aware of a wave of sound rising in the arena.

Ja! Ja! Ja! Ja!

Almost unaware of herself, she joined in, her body moving in time with the chant.

Ja! Ja! Ja!Ja!

It was euphoric. The mob energy, the deafening noise, the strange vibration in her body. She moved rhythmically, again and again, again and again, and suddenly felt her body folding up in long shudders deep inside. It was as if she were in an earthquake, not in control of herself. It was as if she was riding the waves of a thundering river, and the waves were within her. It was strange, it was exhilarating. Finally, as her body calmed down, she stopped moving and held on to the railings, eyes closed and heart still thudding hard, then finally straightened up and looked around with new eyes. The world was the same, the crowds were still shouting, the air was thick with dust and the smell of sweat. But she felt different. Hiba touched her body through the side slit of the gown and found that she was drenched in sweat.

She turned to her companions who were still cheering the roosters on.

'Let us go.'

On the way back, she sat quietly in the cart, looking out at the lights of the city.

What happened to me back there? Did the first real excitement of my life bring on that reaction? Did I experience at last the pleasure of life that all women speak of but have rarely experienced? If that is true, I want more such evenings, I want them every day ...

Her mother was waiting for her in her chamber. She frowned disapprovingly as Hiba came in, head gear thrown back, revealing a flushed face.

'*Really*, Hiba! I heard you had gone to indulge in a ... a ... disgusting *peasant* pastime!'

Hiba ignored her tone and waited for her to continue.

'I came here today to give you one good news and one bad.'

'Well?'

'The good news is that Adham has sent me a message that he is enchanted with the gift I had sent him and plans to come and claim the real thing. And the bad news ...' she paused. 'The bad news is that Baz and Roopmati have been together for the last four days and four nights. He has neglected all his royal duties and lies in her arms, day and night.'

Hiba did not flinch. She looked her mother in the eye. '*Ammi*, I don't care. Let him do what he wants. I plan to live my life as I want from now onwards. I don't need a man to make me complete.'

Chapter 25

For the first time in his life, Adham Khan was besotted by a woman. Not even a flesh and blood woman, but the likeness of her, created by a master painter, to captivate him as no sport ever had, to intoxicate him as the finest wines in the land could not.

He sat for hours, gazing at Roopmati's portrait. In fact, he had done little else since the parcel had arrived from Mandu a few days back.

Palace minions had conveyed the news of the arrival of the work of art to Adham's wife, Begum Javeda, in the women's quarters. The news had travelled by mouth from the security guards to Adham's personal chaprasi to the chaprasi's wife in the zenana. The short, portly maidservant waddled, hips swaying like a large bundle of cloth, down long corridors and open courtyards until she reached the doors of Javeda Begum's rooms where she lived with her young sons, her unmarried sister and an old aunt. Panting audibly, the woman pushed the door open and went in. She looked in the chambers and finding them unoccupied, went out into the sunny courtyard. Javeda was sitting there, getting her hair oiled and her feet massaged as her children played with pebbles and her aunt talked droningly as she bent over some embroidery she was doing.

'Begum Saheba, Begum Saheba!' The maid was breathless from the exertion of carrying breaking news to her mistress. Javeda opened her eyes and studied her disinterestedly. There was very little that had excited her for years now.

'Begum Saheba, there is something you must know! A parcel arrived for Adham Khan Saheb a short while ago. He unwrapped it and found that it was a painting of a beautiful woman. He placed it in his chamber and ever since, he has been gazing at it!'

Javeda closed her eyes again.

So what is new? If not a woman in the flesh, then the likeness of a woman on a board!

As her aunt asked questions in a quavering voice and the maidservant chattered on, Javeda's mind drifted to a time when she could remember being young and excited and starry eyed. The daughter of Baqi Khan Baqlani, a respected noble of Akbar's court, Javeda would often join the royal women behind the latticed screen of the Emperor's private audience hall to watch court proceedings. Her eyes always lingered on the handsome form of Adham Khan, the Emperor's milk brother, and she began to manipulate her seating position, reaching early to choose a seat from where she had the best view of Adham. Through the filigreed wooden screen, she would drink in his features, his thick black hair and short beard, his broad shoulders and the hair on his arms that glinted gold at the tips. She watched him speak and frown and laugh. And fell head over heels in love with him.

One day, emerging from the cloistered area behind the screen, she saw that her father had not left the diwan-e-khaas hall with the other men. He was standing to one side, near the entrance. Sensing that he was waiting for her, Javeda went up to him and spoke softly through her veil.

'Abbu, is there something you wish to say to me?'

He looked away and nodded. He spoke gruffly.

'Yes. Why the court at your age? What interests you?'

'A courtier, Abbu.'

'Hmm. He is in the close coterie of the Jahanpanah?'

'Yes.'

'Even one wrong move on my side can get our bodies swinging from the highest gallows.'

'Yes.'

'I will speak if you are sure of what you want.'

'Yes.'

He hesitated, then nodded heavily and walked away with slow, loping steps.

Soon it was known that Emperor Akbar had ordered Adham to marry Javeda Khan. The marriage took place in the Emperor's own gardens and afterwards, a resplendent, radiant Javeda followed Adham into his home.

The years have rolled away, leaving me with two children and dark circles under the eyes. Much has changed between us, but so little has changed about him; he has his endless stream of women to keep his bed warm, and I have my endless stream of thoughts to keep my memories alive ...

The painting had become an obsession with Adham. He was not satisfied with the light in his chambers and had chosen a space in his mahal with good lighting and background in the *baramda,* a terrace wrapped on three sides by a lush green garden. He carried the painting there himself and carefully placed it on an easel, angling it to face his armchair. This way, seated in the deep cushioned chair, he could look at it for hours, his eyes sweeping over the curves of Roopmati's face, her long neck, her slim shoulder and her swelling bosom. He sometimes rubbed his jaw as he looked and sometimes licked his lower lip. There was something in the woman that fascinated him, charmed him, excited him. Was it the innocence? No, it may not be; painters were known to add that trait to all their paintings of young women. Was it the appeal to his aesthetic senses? May be. Could it be the smouldering sensuality he sensed below the gentle smile? Yes, definitely. He laughed out loud, the laugh of the victor who knows he will be victorious even before his victory has happened.

Ahh Roopmati! If only you knew what lies ahead! If you but knew that Adham Khan is coming to claim you, you would toss aside that poor fool who has nothing but a crumbling kingdom and a stumbling army to keep himself on the throne! When I walk into Mandavgarh fort, Mughal banners flying, you will see Baz Bahadur on his knees, paying homage to the conqueror of Malwa, Adham Khan!

The bead curtains at the door shook gently.

'Kaun hai?' He demanded, loath to be disturbed in his reverie.

'Huzoor, Jahanpanah Akbar sends a messenger to you.'

Adham Khan sat up immediately. 'Let him come.' He quickly drew a red velvet cloth down over the painting.

The Emperor's messenger came in and bowed.

'The Emperor orders that you come to him immediately in his private chambers.'

'Very well. You may go.'

Adham hurriedly dressed and left for Akbar's palace. As he walked across the vast courtyards of the fort, passing well laid-out Afghan gardens, and mosques and pavilions built in the Persian style, his mind was perplexed. What could Akbar want with him suddenly? They had already discussed the campaign for the capture of Malwa in the War Council meeting. Had he heard about the portrait that had arrived from Mandu and his, Adham's obsession with it? If news of Roopmati had spread, Akbar may decree that Roopmati should not be touched when the fort is taken, thus rendering Adham's whole idea of war on Baz Bahadur meaningless.

Adham's heart was beating fast as he was ushered into Akbar's private chamber. The Emperor had his mother, Hamida Begum, the late Humayun's queen and now Queen Mother, seated beside him. They were both laughing and turned and looked at Adham welcomingly.

'Come, my milk brother, be seated,' said Akbar after the initial greetings were over. '*Ammi* and I were talking about the renovations that are required to be done in the fort. We may have won this great land from Ibrahim Lodi and again wrested it back from Sher Shah Suri, but alas, this dilapidated fort we have inherited from them is indeed a disgrace!' He laughed with good humour and Adham smiled cautiously.

'Adham, as we discussed in the War Council yesterday, our Army will be ready to march into Malwa within a couple of weeks and after defeating the Sultan's armies, onwards to Gondwana. But I shall not be able to go to war this time. The time is not right, because I have drawn up detailed plans with my teams of builders and architects for the renovation, and my presence is required here during that period.' He paused and looked at Hamida Begum.

'*Ammi* feels, you will be able to handle the campaign this time along with our stalwart commanders and generals. And, of course, Ahmad Khan is always there to guide and support you.'

Adham felt as if a huge boulder had rolled off his chest. He laughed out aloud.

'Jalal, my brother! Of course, you are right! You need to be here to approve the rebuilding works. And *Ammijaan,*' he turned to Hamida, 'Rest assured that this other son of yours too shall keep the green silk banner flying as high as your real son always has!'

Chapter 26

Hiba was a new person. The experience at the cock fighting ring had left her weak in the knees and strangely craving for more such nights. She had never thought that she would be so much at home in an unruly crowd, but apparently she had never really known her true self. She smiled ironically. After all these years of believing that all she wanted was Baz, she had had a revelation. What she really wanted was the excitement and thrill of living, of blood sports, of betting on them. And something else she experienced in the arenas, she couldn't put a finger on it. She smiled at herself in the mirror before pulling the burkha into place.

Her maidservants had been engaged in taking her to explore all the night activities in Mandu—gambling on cards, on dice, on the horn-locking of rams and of course on cock fighting. With Nasi's help, she dressed up every night in coarse clothes and veil, and left stealthily through a side door with her companions. She would press coins into the girls' hands and they would all place their bets after studying the prospects. As always, the tempo would build up, and the cheering and rhythmic chanting would fill the arena and her senses, and Hiba would invariably come back to the palace, satiated and tranquil. Winning bets was never important. The experience of mob energy was.

Nasi watched her mistress with concern. She was becoming too fond of the night outings. It was dangerous; there were hooligans around in the seamy parts of the fort city that they frequented. If it ever came out that the Sultana Begum was being taken to the arenas every night, the girls would be caught and punished. If not by the Sultan, surely by his mother-in-law.

The servant girls began to connive among themselves to find another way of keeping Hiba happy. One evening, as Hiba undressed, shedding her fine clothes for the cheap ones, Nasi opened the door a crack and peeped in.

'Huzoor, I want to bring in a friend to meet you, if you permit me.'

Hiba watched as a stunning woman, much older than her, was led in. She was tall and fair, with a proud, high cheek-boned face and long, lustrous brown hair. She wore a deep-cut flowing dress of indeterminate origin. 'This is Gaaya, Huzoor. She is from Roos; she along with a band of expert *maalishwalis* travelled down from Agra a few weeks ago on hearing that we have a wonderful life in Mandu every evening. She is skilled in massage techniques and I thought you may wish to try her out.'

'But ...' Hiba looked annoyed. 'But Nasi, we were just getting ready to go out!'

'Shh, Huzoor, she does not understand our language but is very sensitive. She may leave if she feels unwanted.'

'But I do *not* want a massage now!' Hiba turned to tell the foreigner off and stopped abruptly. Gaaya was already setting up her shop, it seemed. She lit scented candles and placed them around the room, on tables and ledges and shelves. She laid out jars of creams and coloured oils. She removed her bracelets and rings one by one under their fascinated eyes, and dropped them into a soft leather pouch. Then she reached behind and undid her long dress which slithered to the ground, revealing a satin slip of the same length. Hiba stared at the curve of her magnificent breasts and the flat stomach, creamy pale skin and painted red lips.

'What? Nasi!' She turned to question Nasi, but she was gone, door shut firmly behind her.

Gaaya indicated the bed with a little bow. Hiba stepped gingerly forward, her mind still on the ram fight she was planning to attend that night. Gaaya bent and scooped her up, deposited her on the bed and picking up two jars of cream, climbed in after her and drew the muslin curtains of the four poster bed.

Hours later, Nasi tiptoed in as Gaaya left fully dressed, carrying her bags packed with pots and jars again. 'Huzoor?' She whispered. Hiba was sleeping so soundly that she did not hear. The maidservant peeped in, saw her mistress's pale body sprawled in abandon on the sheets, smiled and crept out again.

Hiba became addicted to Gaaya and Nasi became her night time manager, slowly reducing the outings and bringing Gaaya in more often.

'Soon,' she promised, 'I will bring in another woman to you. She is Farsi, from Persia, and a beauty. She will teach you new

new things. She and Gaaya, together; they don't understand each other, but they will understand you!'

Hiba smiled with secret anticipation, for she now lived for the nights; she couldn't believe that they had once stretched unbearably, alternately yearning for Baz and ranting against his indifference.

Soon Gaaya and Batasha became a regular part of her life, coming in six times a week. They would all three lock themselves into the chamber and the two foreign women would leave at daybreak, all smiles as they collected the pouches of silver coins from Nasi outside the door.

'Seventh day, Huzoor, you rest! Too much pleasure's not good for the body,' said Nasi with a naughty wink at Hiba in the mirror as she brushed her curly locks.

Hiba looked away, embarrassed. Then she forced herself to meet the girl's eyes with a sheepish smile.

'Thank you, Nasi. I know, I have been very hard on you over the years, but you understand ...'

'Yes, I understand, Huzoor. Now you have so much to wait all day for! Correct?'

Hiba laughed, a rare laugh showing pearly teeth.

'But my mother should never, ever know, remember. If she comes here at the wrong time ...'

'I will manage her, Huzoor, don't worry! She will not find out.'

As if on cue, the door was pushed open and Jana Begum walked in. She looked suspiciously at her daughter. 'Where were you last evening? This servant woman told me you had gone to learn music.'

'Yes, *Ammijaan,* I am now a student of Iskar Khan, who had once taught the Sultan himself. I go regularly for singing classes.'

'At that late hour?'

'What to do, *Ammi,* the man has no other time to spare! I am a very bad student, you see, so he has to spend special time with me.'

Jana Begum grunted dismissively. 'Hmm. As long as you don't go for any of those rowdy sports that these girls took you for once.'

Hiba shook her head, eyes wide and innocent.

'No, I don't have a taste for it, I found.'

'Well, anyway, I came to tell you that your husband is not just a foolish lover, but also a foolish ruler.'

Hiba shrugged. She had no more interest in Baz's life.

'Why, what happened?'

'The Mughal Army has set out for Malwa. They are 60,000 strong. The spies have informed our ministers. But Baz Bahadur has not woken from his mistress's embrace yet!'

Hiba frowned with sudden concern.

'Has Baz not ordered his forces to be ready?'

Jana shook her head with a paan-stained sneer.

'No, no, he has not even agreed to meet his council of ministers yet! Adham Khan and his army will be here in about a week's time. Once unchallenged on the plains, they will come up and charge the fort.'

Hiba clutched her throat.

'And?'

'Don't worry, daughter. They have been told to loot whatever there is in the treasury and take away only one prize from here. Roopmati.'

Hiba screamed, a short, agonised scream. 'But why?'

Jana Begum frowned and came up to place a palm on Hiba's brow.

'Are you all right? You sound very distraught. '

'But why abduct Roopmati?' shouted Hiba again. Her eyes were wide and desperate.

'Have you forgotten? To leave the Sultan alone for you of course.'

With another scream, Hiba almost doubled over, hands over her face.

'But I don't want him!'

'Of course, you want him. You have always wanted him.'

'No! I told you a few weeks back that I don't care what Baz does, I don't want him back, ever! I meant it. I really do want to live my life as I please. I don't care about him! And now you have ...' She burst into sobs.

Jana Begum looked around, bewildered.

'What has happened to her?' she demanded of Nasi hovering at the door.

Hiba sobbed as if her heart would break.

'Oh *Ammi*, I don't know whether to blame you or me! This should never have happened! Now the Mughal army will charge our city, plunder everything, leave our life in ruins! And that too, when I have just made a new life for myself! They will kill and rape and torture and leave everything reduced to rubble.

And for what? To give Baz back to me? Oh, Baz was never mine, and never will be!'

She turned a tear-stained face to her mother. 'It is all my fault. When you planned and plotted to have Roopmati taken away from here, I kept quiet. When you sent her portrait to Adham Khan, I kept quiet. Call it my foolishness, call it my delusional thinking. How did I ever think Baz would come back to me then? The truth is, if Roopmati left, he would have gone to his concubines! Never to me!' She wept again.

Jana Begum watched her grimly; then turned to Nasi.

'When my daughter comes back to her senses, tell her that as soon as news comes of the Mughal army riding up to Mandu, all women and children of this palace will go into the secret passages and hide in the rooms below the *baolis*. Pass this word around.'

Chapter 27

Roopmati was back in Baz Bahadur's Palace, and now their *mehfils* had no other musicians or singers or audience. Baz would not have anyone else listening to her. She sang for him, and they sang together in the Rang Mahal, in the pavilion overlooking the garden, in the courtyard and in their bed chamber. They sang the ragas of joy, of awakening, of fulfilment. There was no place in their lives for the sad songs of parting and desertion and death. Because life could not get any more beautiful.

Until it all began to fall apart.

They were on the terrace of the pavilion, from where Roopmati gazed on the Narmada every day. It was late winter and the afternoon sun had ripened the air to a warm golden sweetness. Roopmati lay on her stomach on a silk rush mat, while he sat next to her, rubbing scented oil onto her back. She closed her eyes, her every nerve pinpointed to his touch. Even after these past weeks of being together day and night, their heightened pleasure in each other's touch had not dimmed.

She buried her face in her folded arms and hummed a snatch of a ghazal. He stopped massaging her and laughed.

'So, my classical queen, the charm of a ghazal has rubbed off on you at last, I see?'

She rolled over and drawing her discarded sari near to cover herself, lay looking up at him,

'Hmm. May be it is just you who have rubbed off on me!' she whispered.

She held the cloth tight as his hand slipped below it.

'Well, I would be surprised if I hadn't. After all, this constant touching should have some effect, don't you think?' His fingers were mischievous.

She squealed and wrapping her sari around her, jumped up and ran to the edge of the terrace. There, her open tresses blowing in the mellow breezes of the season, she looked down towards his palace by the waters of the Rewa Kund, its stately, gracious lines, the two courtyards, one behind the other, and the terrace ending in Afghan styled cupolas.

He came up behind her and encircled her waist with his muscular arms.

'Baz,' she asked thoughtfully, 'How does the water come up from the *kund* into your palace? It flows into your pool in the courtyard and in the channels that run through all your rooms, doesn't it?'

'Hmmm. An intelligent question from a mere woman!'

'What did you say?' She whirled around indignantly.

'Well,' he pretended to look apologetic, but his eyes were shining wickedly. 'Most women would have thought the pool gets filled by rows of women walking into the palace with pots on their heads!'

She suppressed a gurgle of laughter at the image and tried to look stern.

'Stop insulting women, Baz, and answer my question. How does the water climb up from the lake?'

He released one arm from around her and pointed to the passage leading from the entrance steps into the first courtyard of the palace.

'Can you see a wooden wheel system on the roof of the passage? Well, that is a Persian wheel. We call it *saqiya*. It has a lever that is turned by a man standing on top. That turns another wheel that sends a chain of buckets dipping into the lake to bring up water. The water goes up into a channel that feeds into our pool and all the scented waterways in the rooms. Satisfied, my beautiful one?'

'Hmmm ... ' she considered. 'And when is this done?'

'Whenever I am ready to swim or bathe, Ahmed *miya* sends a man up.'

He lifted her chin. 'Roopmati, you are not just beautiful and talented, but intelligent too. I cannot wait to create beautiful children just like you.'

She shook her head and opened her lips to speak, but he had already covered them with his own.

~

Baz and Roopmati enjoyed walking together in the garden at sunset. Here, near the southern wall, it was a different Mandu from that of the complexes of mahals around the Munj Talab. Here, the evening withdrew gently to the music of birdsong and the night slid quietly into the cacophony of crickets. Here, the palaces did not light up the waters with a thousand shaking lights; the sky sprinkled starlight into the courtyard pool and sank its black cloak into the Rewa Kund.

I thought that was magical. But how much more beautiful is this silence and the solitude and the presence of Baz at my side!

They talked. And they discussed. And they sparred.

Baz had begun to discover that Roopmati was nothing like the women of his harem. While she could be soft and yielding in love, she had a strong sense of her identity too, being proud of her simple background and yet, filled with humility when she spoke of her father and her guru and how they had shaped her mind and her music.

'They taught me that being a woman does not mean I am only what my body can do ... cook and clean and bear children and look decorative for a man. They taught me to be a person in my own right, and to express my thoughts, my opinions, my needs as much as a man.'

Baz gazed at her in fascination. The women of his family and his concubines, his singing and dancing girls ... they only lived to snare a man and hold him in their power for money and jewels and gold.

'For me,' continued Roopmati, as if she had read his mind, 'a given word is more precious than all the wealth in the land.'

'Yes,' he said slowly. 'I realised that when I wanted to bring you here with me. You refused, and finally agreed only on one condition.'

She smiled. 'I think I started to fall in love with you when I saw that you kept your word, no matter how challenging it was.'

He gave a short bark of laughter.

'Ask me, and I'll tell you how challenging it was! I had promised myself that I would not touch you until ...'

'Until?' she asked mischievously.

'Until you surrendered to me yourself.'

Roopmati stopped walking and turned to him, brows drawn together and arms folded across her chest in indignation.

'Surrender? I *surrendered* to you?'

He hid a smile. 'Yes, like those women in Jahaz Mahal do to the men who chase after them.'

Roopmati twirled on her heel and was walking away when her arm was caught and she was yanked back into his arms. He held her and nuzzled the top of her head.

'Like I'm surrendering to you now. Do what you want with me.'

She remained silent. He lifted his arms and peeped into her face.

'All yours.'

Roopmati gave a ripple of laughter, then sobered down.

'But Baz, you should not speak of those women like that. They have grown up believing that that is the right way to live.'

'What women? I don't know any other but you.' He looked up at the sky.

'Hmmm ... a dark night. Come, my *jal pari,* the scene is set for us to cavort in the waters together.'

The days and nights began to melt together for Roopmati and Baz. They wrote verses and sang and played and swam and made love as if this here was the whole world and this moment all time.

One evening, Roopmati sat in the dark courtyard, listening to the low rumble of the pulley on the roof and the water of the Rewa Kund going up, running along channels over the first square, then to their private courtyard and finally, splashing down into the pool. She enjoyed the few moments of solitude, while Baz was inside writing at his desk. She looked around at the arched entrances, the granite statues, the slender pillars meeting in graceful arches. Living within these walls, cocooned in love, she had forgotten the other worlds she had come from. Her father's home in Malwa and her home with Sadiya, they seemed so far away, and yet, each of them had been a doorway that led her here. To Baz.

She looked up as he walked out of his chambers, as though her thoughts had drawn him out.

He came up to where she sat dabbling her toes in the water and held out a hand.

'Come, Roopmati. The garden pavilion has been lit up with coloured lamps and sandal incense sticks; I want to sit there and read you a few verses I have written.'

'No, you come sit here and recite them to me.' She patted the floor near her.

He looked around. 'No, the courtyard is too cold tonight; even though *Vasant ritu* is almost upon us, the air has not warmed in the evenings. The pavilion has been carpeted with thick rugs and soft cushions in preparation for an evening of my favourite things: wine, poetry and music, and you.'

She laughed. 'Really? *Things*? You make me sound like an object.'

'Well, you are. You belong to me.'

She leapt up and ran to the other side of the pool. 'Take that back or I will jump into the pool and stay there all evening!'

'I will jump in and carry you out!'

'Like you did that first time? Huh! Just try it! I will swim away!'

She slid into the water with all her clothes on, then gasping at its coldness, struggled to hold her billowing sari down.

Baz gave a roar of laughter and was just pulling off his clothes when he glanced up and froze. There was the shadow of a man on the roof, looking down into the courtyard. Quick as a sliver of lightning, Baz pulled out a dagger from his waist and leaning back, flung it with all his might. There was a scream of pain and the figure collapsed bellowing and writhing on the roof. Baz walked out of the courtyard and could be heard barking instructions to his servants. Within minutes, it was all over.

He came back and found Roopmati sitting at the side of the pool, holding a large towel around her wet clothes. She was looking down and shivering uncontrollably.

Baz held a hand out to her but she ignored it. He sat on his haunches and tried to lift her chin, but she turned her face away fiercely.

'Don't touch me!' she bit out through gritted teeth.

He took his hand away and studied her face. She looked stubbornly away.

'All right, I will not touch you. But at least, come in and change your wet clothes. We can talk later.'

They walked into the bed chamber in silence; she picked up a fresh set of clothes from her trunk, went behind a screen to change. He waited patiently, sitting on the bed, until she emerged.

'Now, can you tell me why you are so angry with me?' he asked calmly.

'Are you actually asking me? You just killed a man!'

'Yes, it had to be done.'

'Why?'

'Because he is not allowed to come to this courtyard at all. His job is to turn the wheel over the entrance corridor. He had no business coming up to my private courtyard.'

'So you killed him?'

Her eyes were large with disbelief, dark with disappointment.

'Yes.'

She shook her head slowly.

'Don't ever touch me again. I cannot believe I allowed those hands to touch me.'

'Roopmati, I am a warrior. When I face an enemy, I don't exactly hold his hand and ask about his health. I just hit out, with the aim to kill.'

She ran a trembling hand over her face.

'I cannot even kill an ant.'

There was a long silence.

She began to walk towards the door.

'Where are you going?'

'Back to Shahi Mahal. I want nothing more to do with you. We are finished. I will return to my house in Nimar tomorrow.'

'You cannot go to Shahi Mahal at this time of night. Sadiya will not be there, nor Panna now.'

He caught her arm.

'Leave me!' she screamed, her voice uncontrolled. 'I will go anywhere, it does not matter, but I will not stay with you.' She fought him off. 'Tomorrow, if I do something you don't like, may be you will kill me too!'

He picked her up and carried her to the bed and laid her down a little roughly.

Then he leaned over her, his arms on both sides of her, not allowing her to move or get up.

'Roopmati, listen to me!'

She pushed at his chest with all her strength and then rolled over and pulling a pillow to her, hugged it and burst into sobs. Suddenly, she felt very alone, desolate, as if the man she had known and loved had changed so much that she could not recognise him anymore.

She fell asleep as the sobs turned to hiccoughs and then petered out into an exhausted silence.

Baz lay beside her without letting his body touch hers. He could not sleep. His heart twisted with anguish as he thought of the pain in her eyes, her disappointment with him, perhaps even her fear of being with a man who could be so suddenly, physically violent.

I can never let her know, ever, how I killed my own brother for Mandu. She would never look at me again, let alone respect me.

He thought of her beautiful eyes lit up with adoration, her soft hands in his, her very body given so trustingly into his possession.

Have I spoilt it all in one moment of fury? Will she ever trust me again?

With a soft groan, he turned and looked at the back of her head, the loosened plait on the pillow, her vulnerable neck that he had often nuzzled.

He moved forward and gently pressed his lips to the back of her neck and waited. She moved slightly. He smoothed a hand over her head and bending, whispered into her ear, 'Roopmati, I am sorry. Forgive me.'

She stiffened, but did not turn. He sat up and pulled her up into his arms, raining little kisses all over her face.

Roopmati opened swollen eyes and looked at him.

'You are a stranger to me. I don't even know that part of you,' she said. 'I believed you to be kind and sensitive and caring, not a man who will kill for ... for ... a sense of power.'

He shook his head.

'No, that is not why I reacted so suddenly and threw my dagger. It was not to show my power or position.'

She waited, unconvinced.

'The man had drifted into our private courtyard because he knew you were with me. He probably wanted to see you half dressed, or even less, in the pool. It was the primal instinct of an unlettered man that made him take a terrible risk and venture into our private spaces.'

She looked at him, stunned. It was true, she had been in the pool often, swimming and cavorting with Baz, wearing barely anything, confident in the knowledge that no one, absolutely no one, was allowed to come anywhere near their courtyard without permission. The very thought of being seen by a man other than Baz made her cringe. She covered her face with her hands and spoke through them in muffled tones.

'I ... cannot imagine ...'

'I know. Nor can I. I don't know how this man dared to try this stunt. Anyway, in future, no one else will defy my orders.' His arms tightened around her and he whispered, 'You are my *jal pari* and only mine.' He teased her lips with his, until she surrendered. They made love as never before ... tender yet ardent, slow and tantalising, yet urgent ...

~

In the Hindola Mahal, the ministers were meeting. They sat along both walls, ignoring the empty chair at the head. They were all angry, frustrated, feeling helpless.

'We had information weeks back that the Mughal forces were planning to attack Malwa by the end of winter. The Sultan was informed, but beyond verbal orders to the military commanders to ready our forces, he has done nothing!'

'We have told him time and again that our troops and animals are not in a position to survive an attack. In fact, they cannot defend themselves, leave alone our territories.'

'We are trying to keep their morale high and continuing with training activities, but an army needs weapons and food to fight!'

'Yes, the coffers are almost empty. We had to recompense the peasants and the small traders and buy food grains to tide us over until the next harvest.'

'All rebuilding and public works had to be put aside this year. Except for the royal complexes and their lakes and gardens, the rest of our fort city remains damaged by the rains.'

'All right, now to come to the crux of today's meeting, I had told you all this morning that our spies have reported to me that the Mughal armies have left Agra and are on their way here. Has the Sultan been informed of this?'

'Yes, I went myself to his palace but his staff told me that he was in the Pavilion, on the terrace, with Roopmati.'

'Then?'

'I went up to the Pavilion and found that he had posted guards at the entrance. They refused to allow me entry and also refused to take a message up to him, saying that they had strict instructions not to disturb him.'

There was a long, angry silence. Then the Wazir-e-Azam spoke, trying to stay calm.

'It is now the first watch of the night. Perhaps the Sultan has come back to his palace. I suggest that we all go there and demand an audience with him. This cannot go on any longer. Our very futures are at stake, all Malwa is in danger!'

~

As Baz and Roopmati lay entwined, murmuring sweet nothings, trying to ease the pain they had caused one another, there was a crash of boots in the passage beyond their chamber, on the other side of the courtyard.

'Huzoor!'

Baz went to the door and spoke in a loud voice to carry across the space.

'Leave me alone! I am busy!'

'Huzoor, I have been sent by the Council of Ministers with an urgent message for you,' said the invisible voice.

Roopmati came up behind Baz and looked at him.

He looked towards the entrance, arms akimbo and nostrils flaring. 'What is it?'

'Huzoor, the Council of Ministers wishes to meet you immediately and are waiting for you in your public audience chamber.'

'*Here*?' Baz sounded furious. 'In my palace?'

'Yes, Huzoor.'

There was a long silence. Roopmati said softly, 'Meet them, Baz, perhaps it is something very important.'

He shook his head. 'I am tired of these ministers. All they want to do is meet, meet, meet! What new thing can they have to tell me? The treasury is depleted, the peasants are homeless, the crops have failed, and oh yes, the army is ailing!'

'Baz,' Roopmati pleaded. 'Please go and meet them. I have a bad feeling. Perhaps something *is* seriously wrong.'

Baz threw his hands up impatiently and strode back into his chambers. Roopmati stood looking out thoughtfully at the water of the pool rippling in the starlight. Had Baz been neglectful of his duties? Did the ministers have good reason to demand this interview of him? What had happened? What was going to happen?

~

In the main hall of public audience, the ministers stood around Baz seated in a deep armchair. Roopmati stood near a pillar, trying to make herself as inconspicuous as possible. Baz had insisted that she attend the meeting.

'You are the future queen of Malwa and I need them to accept you as such.' he had said.

The ministers explained one by one that in the past weeks, Adham Khan's army had made full preparations for war. They had now left Agra for Malwa, soldiers and archers, muskets and canons, horses and elephants. The columns were advancing steadily day by day, and would be here in less than a week.

'Get our army ready!' said Baz. 'What is our strength?'

'Three thousand to their sixty thousand,' replied the commander of the forces drily.

'What! But how? Why?'

'We talked about it months ago, Huzoor, and I had explained to you that we had a shortage of food and weaponry and war animals. We had to trim our forces down based on these factors.'

The interchange continued, Baz shooting questions and the commanders giving him the raw, unpolished facts. Roopmati listened, her heart sinking with shame and regret. Baz had forgotten the world for her; his responsibilities, his duties, his very kingdom.

With a choking sob, she slipped out of the door and ran down the passages all the way to their chamber. Then she sank down on the bed and dried her tears with trembling hands. Baz loved her so much that he had left everything else. Now she would show him how much she loved him. With determination, she stood up and looked around for paper and quill. She wrote and pinned the note to his *achkan* and hurried from the room down some steps into a garden and out from there to where a palki was permanently parked for her.

'The Shahi Mahal,' she said and her voice was strong again.

Chapter 28

She was strong again.

The months of madness, the weeks of weakness were over. No, love could not be allowed to rule everything in the world. Baz had lost his balance for some time, but she would help him find himself again too. Even if it meant the end of the enchanted world they had created for themselves.

Back in Shahi Mahal, Roopmati faced an agitated Sadiya.

'Sadiya, the time has come for us to part ways,' she said. 'I am leaving for the plains, going back to my home in the Nimar valley.'

'But why, Bibijaan? Why? If you and the Sultan have had a quarrel, don't worry, all will be well soon. Lovers' fights never last!' She winked and quoted mischievously. 'As Rumi wrote, "Love finally is its own relief ... first bitter and spicy, but finally sweet!" After all, the best part of a fight is making up afterwards, isn't it, Bibijaan?'

Roopmati thought of the night before and all that had happened, and laughed shyly.

'Yes,' she said. 'But don't worry, Sadiya, it is not because the Sultan and I have fought. I want to leave Mandu, because the time has come for the Sultan to mobilise his armies and fight the Mughals who are approaching fast. He needs to be free of my presence so that he can concentrate on the military campaign. Please, Sadiya, understand my agony and my guilt! Help me to make my way back home!'

'All right, Bibijaan, but on two conditions.'

'What are they?'

'First, that you will not travel alone.'

'But who can accompany me at this time?'

'I will. We will go in a palki together and after leaving you in your house, I will return to Mandu.'

'And?'

'And you will promise to come back to Mandu, to the Sultan once the enemy forces retreat.'

Roopmati smiled and nodded. 'Yes, I will. I will come back to Baz, but only after he has done his duties as a ruler and a protector of his people.'

Outside the window, they heard a commotion. Looking out, they saw people running on the roads. There was the distant beat of war drums, and the blast of trumpets, the neighing of horses. 'Panna, Panna!' shouted Sadiya. 'Where are you? Come in immediately!'

Panna came in without his characteristic swagger. For once he looked terrified.

'Panna, what is going on in the streets? There is so much noise and confusion.'

'Yes, I heard that the Sultan has called for army action. The archers, musketeers and war horses in Mandu will leave immediately for the plains. The elephants, camels, canons and foot soldiers will be mobilised from Dhar and all the forces will assemble at Sarangpur to confront the Mughal armies as they march southwards.'

Roopmati held her cheeks.

'Oh, then we must make haste, Sadiya!'

'Yes, Bibijaan, but we cannot leave in the midst of all the chaos! There will be hundreds of horses and soldiers on the roads of Mandu. Our palki cannot go through.'

Roopmati fought down the feeling of panic and drew a few deep breaths.

'You are right, of course. Let us wait until the army moves out and then make our way to the gate.'

They stood together at the window, watching the streets of Mandu churning with people and noise. Sadiya pointed out, 'These are wholesale merchants in the fanned *safas*. They are hastening to barricade their granaries and storage rooms. Then those are small traders, such as we see in the bazaar street, you can recognise them by their dhotis and short kurtis. Then the peasants, the manual labourers, the domestic helpers, the eunuchs for the royal complex—they are all here in the crowds rushing to secure their homes, their families, their possessions.'

'Will they stay on in Mandu, you think?'

'No, Bibijaan, many of them are running to escape. They will try to slip out of the gate before the army comes charging out, but will not be very successful. They have old people, children, the ill and the handicapped with them, so; taking them to the plains will be impossible.'

'So ... when ... *if* the enemy forces charge our fort, what will happen to them?'

Sadiya shook her head sadly.

'Anything could happen. They will be looted, beaten, raped, even killed. Hence, the panic everywhere.'

Roopmati stood very still, thinking. Then she asked, 'What about the women of the royal complex? The royal family, the concubines, the maidservants, the companions?'

Sadiya looked around and lowered her voice.

'There is a place for them to go to in such times. Secret passages leading down from each palace and mahal to chambers below the *baolis*. These step wells are so well concealed that even if enemy soldiers go down the *baoli* steps to drink water, they will never find them. Only we know of the entrances to these honeycomb chambers and they are a closely guarded secret.'

'So the women and children will be safe?'

Sadiya nodded. 'Yes. Bibijaan, there is a secret passage below us too, from the Shahi Mahal to the *baoli*, that you must escape to if the need arises.'

Roopmati did not reply. They stood a long, long time at the window, until the clarion calls died down.

'The army has left,' said Sadiya, and Roopmati felt a great sense of sadness settle upon her. So Baz had left for war. He had not come to meet her one last time, not even for a fleeting meeting of the eyes through this very window.

There is no use in yearning for a last glimpse of him; it is how I wanted it.

She sat curled up on the floor of her room, as she had, on that first night in Mandu to write verses on the enchanting night she witnessed outside. But now, she wrote slowly, sadly, in her notebook:

My heart for thy heart ever longs,
My lips for thy lips ever yearn,
My ears for thy sweet word of wife
On thy return.

The palki wound its way through crowds that had thinned on the roads now. Roopmati looked around at Mandu as they bounced along, and it was like leaving her *sasural* for her *maika*. While the thought of being back in her childhood home was exciting, leaving Mandu wrenched her heart. This is where she had lived as a woman, albeit for a very short time. She could not bear to be away very long.

I pray that Baz and his armies repel the enemies and come back home victorious. And then when he comes to claim me again, I shall return home a proud wife and queen.

She smiled to herself all the way to the main gate of the fort. Finally, the palki stopped and was lowered down. Sadiya looked out and exclaimed in dismay.

'What is it?' Roopmati craned her neck to see the gate. The massive teakwood double gate with its iron frames and spikes was firmly closed and barred and chained across with heavy iron.

The palki bearers were speaking to the contingent of guards near it. The chief of the guards came back to where Sadiya and Roopmati waited.

'Huzoor, we are very sorry, but the gates have been closed for security reasons. No one can go out or come into Mandu without the Sultan's orders.'

'Which means, until the battle is over!' exclaimed Sadiya.

He nodded and bowed himself away.

Sadiya turned to Roopmati with concern.

'I am so sorry, Bibijaan, we cannot go down to Nimar!'

Roopmati nodded. 'It is all right, Sadiya. Let us go back.' She felt no disappointment, just a calm sense of duty, like there was some mission to be accomplished.

As the palki bearers came to a fork where one path led to the southern complex and the other back to the royal complex, Roopmati leaned out of the opening and said to the bearers, 'Can you please turn left here? I want go to the Rewa Kund first.'

Roopmati stood in the water and paid silent homage to the Narmada at the lake that had once sprung from the river far below, then walked up the hillock to her viewing pavilion. There, on the terrace, sari fluttering in the cool spring breezes, she and Sadiya stood and looked at the silver thread of river in the distance.

'Come, Bibijaan, let us go back to the Shahi Mahal,' said Sadiya.

Roopmati shook her head with a smile. 'No.'

Sadiya looked at her, puzzled.

'What do you mean? We should return now.'

'No Sadiya, I am not going.'

'Bibijaan,' begged the little woman, 'Please, come now. Soon it will be evening and then too dark to stay up here by ourselves.'

'You go, Sadiya, I will not leave this spot, until Baz comes back safe or until the enemies enter Mandu.'

'But why!'

'Because, Sadiya, from here I can see right down to the plains. That is where the fighting armies will reach as the battle progresses. I will be able to see everything from up here. I will know who is the victor by seeing the forces that ride up to the fort gates.' She pointed along the wall, 'There, do you see? That is the main gate there. I will see who enters Mandu after the battle, the Sultan's men, or the Emperor's.'

There was a long, ominous silence as the implications of what she had just said sank into her companion's mind.

She turned to ask her mistress what it would mean if, and what *if* ... but did not have the courage to do so. She merely nodded. They stood in a deep silence watching the river with its unchanging destiny.

Chapter 29

Seated on a makeshift stool, Baz Bahadur buried his head in his hands as yet another runner left his tent. The tidings were not good. In fact, they were devastating. Baz shook his head, angry and frustrated.

'More of our soldiers have fled! Joined the Mughals in their fight against us. Traitors! Traitors! They shall be caught and tried and hung for treason.'

Even as he raved and ranted, he knew there was nothing he could do. His forces had fallen into disarray just hours after they were attacked by the Mughal army near Sarangpur, early in the morning. With old, outdated and inefficient weaponry and poor morale, the soldiers succumbed to the lure of money and position in the enemy lines. The horses, most in poor health, could not keep up with the demands of battle and collapsed, leaving the cavalrymen exposed to musket fire. The elephants, though not many in number, were the only combatants on the battle field now.

In the tent, where Baz had come to take quick stock of his losses, the atmosphere was tense. As the wounded, groaning or screaming in pain, were tended to at the back, Baz's general threw a hastily drawn map over a supplies bag in the corner and pointed with a stick.

'Huzoor, these are our only defences left now. A handful of archers, musketeers on 16 elephants and about 40 horsemen with swords. The canons fell silent an hour back. There are no more soldiers to fire them. But even as we speak, all these numbers are dwindling!'

Baz caught his lower lip in his teeth and raked through his thick hair with both hands.

What has happened? How did all this happen? My army ... it's falling to the enemy's attack as if it is a game with wooden soldiers and horses! It cannot be ... we cannot suffer defeat at the hands of the Mughal forces ... no, never! Losing to Adham Khan can only mean one thing ... losing Roopmati! No, no, never!

Baz stamped around the tent, breathing hard and considering every action that could possibly be taken. He was angry, so angry with himself, with his troops, with Adham Khan. And yes, with Roopmati for having left him with a single line scrawled on paper.

Let strife be your guiding force, not love. The kingdom is bigger than you and I.

Finally, having come to a decision, he stopped pacing and glared at the general who stood awaiting his orders.

'I hate to say this, but there is no choice. You are all free to go! Run away or join the enemy, do whatever you wish. Each man to his own now! Pass the word around!' He turned and walked out of the tent, his back straight and angry.

As he walked away from the battle field, he closed his senses to the sounds in the background ... the clash and ring of metal on metal, the neigh of horses, the sounds of gunshots and the cries of the wounded.

He knew what he had to do.

Roopmati had not moved from her post since the previous afternoon. She stood under the Afghan-styled dome of the pavilion at the end of the terrace and gazed down untiringly. From this height, the Nimar valley looked patchily green, its forests a darker shade and the meadows lighter. Her gaze was fixed on the open fields, where she knew the armies would charge as they came in fighting from Sarangpur.

Sadiya was curled near her feet, half asleep. Exhausted from the vigil, she had lain down some time back, but opened her eyes occasionally to check on her mistress.

As Roopmati watched the distant ground, she saw a slow movement building, like ants gathering, moving, marching, ceaselessly. They began to move en masse towards the rise of the hill. The green silk banners were unmistakable.

She straightened up and called out to her companion, 'Come, Sadiya, it is time to go.' Her loyal companion stood up unquestioningly. They walked hand in hand down the stone stairway, down the grassy slope to the palki.

Roopmati knew what she had to do.

The elephants had begun pushing at the gates. They had uprooted tall trees and now used them to shove the trunks against the massive doors, again and again, to the wild war whoops of Mughal soldiers. Deep in the fort city of Mandu, the people trembled in their homes, their hiding holes, their secret passages, as the very ground shook to the booming sounds of elephants at the gates.

In the royal complexes, the privileged had opened their trap doors set beneath polished floors and behind wall murals and between walls, and escaped down dark tunnels to settle into hiding chambers below the huge wells of Mandu. But these places could take only so many; the trap door often crashed cruelly in the desperate faces of those not deemed important.

In Jal Mahal Jana Begum supervised the evacuation of the womenfolk of the palace with severe precision. She stood sentinel as Nasi rounded up all the royal family members, women and children, and having sent them down, finally crouched down to enter the chamber herself. But Jana Begum laid a thick arm over the entrance.

'No more place inside,' she said flatly. Nasi's eyes filled with tears and she clasped her hands in desperation. But Jana Begum was unrelenting.

'The place can take only 20, and we already have 32. Do you want us all to die of suffocation?' As Nasi watched, she managed to push her body through and slammed and fastened the trap from inside.

Nasi jumped up and ran all the way around the Munj Talab to the Jahaz Mahal along with other maidservants and cooks and cleaners of the palaces. Perhaps they could be accommodated in hiding places there.

As they ran up the long straight stairway and breathlessly burst into the main hall, they saw women running behind pillars, ducking behind curtains, and even hiding themselves below piles of carpets and cushions. Many were crouching in the pavilions overlooking the Talab, ready to jump into the water and drown if necessary. The distant booming sounds set off wave upon wave of sobs and stifled wails through the chambers.

In Shahi Mahal, there was a deep silence. Roopmati sat in her room and held the note book once given to her by Baz on her lap. She rifled through the pages, reading the poems, softly humming the songs she had set to music. She seemed lost in another world, one of peace and tranquillity, and completely unaware of the commotion outside.

Sadiya stood by the door. Her eyes shone with unshed tears.

'Please, Bibijaan, I beg you, come down to the trap door and hide yourself. Everyone else has gone into the secret chambers below. We are only waiting for you. The Mughals are cruel people when it comes to the women and children of their enemies. You will not be spared.'

Roopmati looked at Sadiya and smiled.

'Go, Sadiya, go in. I would not want you to be in danger of any kind. I wish to be here, because Baz will come back. You see, we did not say goodbye.'

Sadiya opened her mouth to speak, but no one would ever know what she was about to say, because at that moment there was a tremendous sound, like a clap of thunder, of the distant fort gate splintering and collapsing under the onslaught of three elephants. Renewed screams from the roads and the palaces around mingled with the drum beat of the hooves of hundreds of horses, getting louder and louder, appearing to shake the very foundations of the palace. Roopmati and Sadiya clung together instinctively. Through the window, they could see soldiers riding by, shouting to each other, some of them stopping, asking for directions. Suddenly a group of them who had stopped in front of Shahi Mahal to yank a trembling Panna by the scruff of his neck, spoke to him harshly. There was an exchange of words, again and again ... the soldiers shouting and Panna whimpering, the soldiers questioning and Panna replying, until finally it ended in a clamour of triumphant voices and gestures in the direction of the palace. They kicked the eunuch away and wheeling their horses around, galloped away.

More and more soldiers had spread themselves all over the fort city and their loud voices, shouts and bawdy laughter were soon replaced by the sounds of gunshots, blood curdling screams and the endless howls of women.

Sadiya had stopped begging her mistress to hide herself. She sat on the floor near the bed, her head close to Roopmati's lap and her cold hands held in hers. They waited. They knew something was about to happen ...

Adham Khan reined in his jet black Arab stallion and it stood, stamping its hooves impatiently and shaking its head, making the bridle jingle noisily. Entering the main gateway, he had allowed all his troops to gallop into the fort looking for loot and women. But he himself had only one thing on his mind; one prize to carry back to Agra. Roopmati. He looked around, shading his eyes, wondering where in this vast city she would be hidden. He would wait; it was not his best trait, but wait he would, while his crack team of security guards unearthed her whereabouts and reported to him.

In an hour's time, the commander was back, galloping furiously, with a triumphant look on his face.

'Huzoor!' he cried out. 'Huzoor, I have found the woman! She lives in a palace called Shahi Mahal and she is very much present there now! Come, I will lead you to her!'

Adham kicked his horse's flanks and followed the guard. They rode into the complex of palaces and finally stopped in front of Roopmati's mahal.

'This is the house, Huzoor. She is inside. I have the eunuch's word for it. He knows that if he lies, I will have him hung up by his thumbs.'

Adham looked around at the palaces and their gardens and their fountains and pools, delaying and savouring the moment when he would finally see Roopmati in the flesh.

Baz rode away from the battleground in Sarangpur, not stopping until the sounds became muffled and indistinct. Then he dismounted and led his horse to a small stream to drink. He bathed his face and arms, washing away the blood, grime and sweat. He had gotten away lightly. He just had a few superficial wounds where swords had clashed close to him, and scrapes and grazes when he had fallen from his horse and rolled to safety.

But there were soldiers in his forces who had been grievously wounded. They had been writhing on the ground when he left the field, crying out in pain or asking for water. He knew he should have stopped to attend to at least a few of them. He should not have run away at all. It was not befitting for a Sultan, the leader of his men, to do so. He scooped up water to drink thirstily, then sat on a rock in pensive mood.

But I had two good reasons to run away. First to go and seek help from a friendly neighbouring kingdom. We cannot fight the Mughals on our own to get back fallen Mandu, I need to approach my allies in Khandesh and Berar and beg them for their help. And second ...

A flash of pain crossed Baz's face. Roopmati. His second reason for running away was Roopmati. He needed to know if she was all right. Had Adham Khan found her? Or had she gone into hiding? How was she? Did she miss him? And did she regret that she had sent him to battle without so much as a goodbye?

With a sudden resolve, Baz jumped onto his horse and rode back to one side of the battleground from where the action had now moved away. Hiding behind a thicket of trees, he observed the dead soldiers lying strewn around like ducks after a hunt. He saw a Mughal army soldier's body near another thicket some thirty feet away. He bent low and made a dash for it. Within minutes, he had stripped the dead man, pulled on his green uniform and was on his horse, galloping up to Mandu.

Adham Khan was ushered into Roopmati's hall of public audience by a smirking Panna. Now that he had understood what was happening, Panna had become very cooperative with the invaders.

Adham Khan waited while Panna knocked loudly on Roopmati's chamber door, looking back at him with girlish giggles.

For several minutes, there was no response, then the door opened very slowly and Sadiya appeared in the small gap, her eyes blood shot and hair dishevelled. She didn't speak, just waited.

Panna wriggled his body in his usual style and said, 'Where is your mistress? Our new master is here. He demands to see Roopmati.'

Sadiya came out and closed the door carefully.

'Huzoor, my mistress is indisposed. May I carry a message to her?'

'Tell her that Baz Bahadur is a coward and has fled the battlefield. I am Adham Khan, the Mughal army chief. I have come to take her back to Agra, dressed in the finest silks and mounted on my caparisoned elephant, to be presented at Akbar's court as his privileged singer and my mistress. She will never lack for wealth or fame, jewels or comforts there. Adham Khan lays down his heart to her.' He bowed slightly and waited.

Sadiya studied him with large, bulging eyes. Then she too bowed and went back, closing the door firmly behind her.

Adham waited and as time passed, became restless. Had he been conned? Was Roopmati in fact in hiding or had she flown the nest long ago? He drew his sword and stepped towards the door when it opened again. Sadiya stood there, her face puffy and her cheeks tear-stained. She spoke in a low, husky voice.

'Huzoor, my mistress sends you her greetings and accepts your proposal with deep gratitude. However, as she is indisposed, she begs your forgiveness and asks that she be allowed time until night to meet you. She will be ready by the second watch of this night and you may come here then to claim her as your own.'

Adham could not believe his luck. Roopmati had accepted him! He would be carrying her back to Agra as his prize catch, much as he had dreamed over the past months. Well, once she was in his mahal of the fort, he would not let Akbar set eyes on her, else his milk brother would surely take her away to his own harem.

He posted guards all around the palace and as he leapt on to his horse to leave, pointed a finger at a fawning Panna.

'Out! I don't want to see your face again when I return!'

Chapter 30

When the evening raga is sung, they say, the birds become quiet in the boughs of trees and the lights come on in the dusking sky. First, the star of the west, Venus ... *shukr tara* ... comes on, and the sun lights it up just before he sinks out of sight. The first star, the brightest star. Then the constellations come up, like chains of light on a Diwali night in Heaven. Raga Yaman Kalyan has the power to do even more. It brings lovers together, at the exact meeting point between day and night.

Roopmati played her tanpura and sang for one last time in Mandu. This time, she sang of parting and desertion and sadness. Her tanpura throbbed in sympathy. Gently, she caressed the burnished wood of its neck and put it away.

'Come, Sadiya, dress me up, for I have to leave for my future home soon.'

Roopmati sat before the mirror as Sadiya combed her long hair into a tumbling cascade and pinned tiny silver and gold stars on the crown of her head. When she finally stood back, Roopmati rose and stood resplendent in the fine white cotton lehenga, choli and dupatta that had been a love gift from Baz so, so long ago, it seemed. Sadiya gazed at her mistress, her eyes bright with love, yet dimmed with sadness.

'Bibijaan, I don't understand. Can you really go to live with that Adham Khan in his mahal in Agra? Can you give your heart, your body, your soul to anyone other than my master, Sultan Baz Bahadur?'

Roopmati held out her arms to Sadiya, who came hesitantly forward to embrace her.

'You have no faith in your friend, your sister, Sadiya? For shame!' Her smile softened the words.

'Then please explain what is in your mind, Bibijaan. What do you plan to do? Where will you go, dressed in these beautiful clothes gifted by my master?'

'I have waited all evening for my Baz, because I know he will come to meet me. But the night is here and we have less and less time. The Mughal *sipahsalar* will arrive to claim me in the second *peher* of the night, Sadiya, there is barely an hour left now. Will Baz reach me before he does? I do not know. '

'Then what will we do?' There was panic in Sadiya's voice.

'Sadiya, can you bring me my puja *thaal* please?'

Sadiya brought it. 'Bibijaan, I really do not think prayers will help us now.'

'Give me a cup.'

Sadiya handed her a small silver cup. Roopmati shook a handful of brown camphor powder into it and added some sesame oil to it from a brass container. She made a paste of the two and placing the cup by her pillow, knelt down to look into Sadiya's face.

'You have been a good friend and sister to me, Sadiya. Tell the Sultan I waited for him, but could not wait any longer. Life is only as long as the wait for the beloved. When the beloved's name on one's breath ceases to evoke a response, the breath ceases too.'

She handed her the precious notebook.

'Tell him I have said my goodbye to him here. We will meet again, somewhere, sometime, soon.'

She slowly consumed the paste in the cup and lay down. Within minutes, her body spasmed and heaved violently, her arms and legs thrashing around. She gasped for breath again and again and her eyes rolled back in their sockets. Finally, her body shook one last time and then stilled forever.

Sobbing soundlessly, Sadiya lovingly wiped the foam trickling down the corner of her mistress's lips and closed her half-open eyes. She folded her slim hands on her stomach and carefully arranged her dupatta on her body. Then she sat down, head in her hands, to wait.

Baz was on the terrace of the pavilion, holding the slim pillars of the gazebo with his hands as he looked down towards the valley that he could barely discern in the poor light. Night was falling rapidly, and looking at the sky, he could see the first star shining brightly.

Is Roopmati looking at the star too, as she sings the raga Yaman Kalyan?

He had managed to ride into the fort without being accosted. The guards had waved him in, seeing the green uniform. There were too many soldiers riding in today for them to take greater note of each. Guessing that Adham

Khan was already inside, and would choose to stay the night in one of the palaces—*maybe even his, the Baz Bahadur mahal*—Baz had climbed up to Roopmati's pavilion, which lay dark and empty. He would stay here until late and then make his way to the Shahi Mahal. If only, Allah willing, she was safe and free!

He lay down on the floor of the terrace and counted the stars. One star caught his eye. It was brighter than the rest, and flashing again and again. Was it part of the constellations? He thought not. What was its name? He didn't know; he had never noticed it before. He suddenly sat up with a deep sense of foreboding. There was an urgent feeling in him that something needed to be done. He studied the sky.

It must be past the first *peher* of the night. It would now be safe to make his way to the Shahi Mahal.

~

'Koi hai!' The peremptory order rang out in the hall of the Shahi Mahal. Sadiya came out of the chamber, but this was a different Sadiya from what Adham Khan had seen in the afternoon. She had pulled herself up to her full height, her gaze was clear and her voice steady.

She looked way, way up at the interloper and said, 'As *salaam alaikum, Huzoor*!'

'Where is Roopmati? Call her out!' he demanded. He had been drinking heavily.

'*Huzoor*, she is in her chamber.'

'Call her out! I have not even seen her in the flesh yet! And to think I came ... came ... out with Ab-kar ... Ab-bar ... *Akbar's* army just to w ... w ...win her! Call her out!'

Sadiya lowered her eyes.

'*Huzoor*, she waits for you in her chamber.'

'What? He stuttered, taken aback. Then it dawned on him. Roopmati was his. At last. His manner changed, there was a swagger in his body, a sneer on his face. 'Of course she waits! After all, I now own her! Out of my way!'

'Yes, *Huzoor*.'

'What are you waiting for? You may go now!'

He strode into the room and the door closed behind him. There was silence from within. Sadiya waited patiently outside the door to hear the sound of his fury exploding.

~

Baz crept in like a fugitive, into the very palace where he had once been feted by his music lovers, where he would hold *mehfils* and *mushairas* with Roopmati, where he and Roopmati had first declared their love for one another.

'Halt! Who goes in?' asked one of the guards on his rounds.

'A soldier of the Mughal army.'

'What is your work?'

'A message from Adham Khan to Roopmati.'

'You may go in.'

He hesitated in the doorway, his eyes sweeping the carpets and the instruments leaning against one wall, the window at the extreme end where Roopmati would do her *riyaz*, unaware of the morning sun on her silken tresses. He pushed open the door of her chamber and waited, then called softly. 'Roopmati?'

Sadiya stumbled to the door and flung herself at his legs, sobbing uncontrollably.

'Sadiya, where is Roopmati? Is she all right?'

Even as he spoke, his eyes fell on her, sleeping soundly on the bed. With a smile of relief, he laid his finger on his lips.

'Hush, Sadiya, you will wake my *sahibaah*. Let her sleep whilst you tell me about the evil Adham Khan. Did he dare come here? Did he try to touch her?'

She nodded her head, then shook it, hiccoughing as she tried to control herself.

'She wai ... wai ... waited for you, *Hu ... zoor*! She knew you would come.'

'Yes, of course, I would come. She sent me to battle without giving me an embrace. I came to take that last kiss from her and to tell her that I will be back soon to win Mandu back and make her my queen.'

He strode to the bed and knelt down. He touched her face, her hands, her neck, then turned unbelievingly to Sadiya.

'Why is she cold?'

He brought his lips down to hers, then drew back in horror.

'There is no breath.'

Sadiya's shoulders were shaking with silent sobs.

'She's gone. Gone, *Huzoor*! She waited for you, *Huzoor*, then it was time for Adham Khan to come here, so she ... she drank poison and ... she's gone.'

Baz slowly straightened up, running his fingers through his hair. Then he dragged his hands over his face, scratching his cheeks, raking at his beard, finally beating his chest as he let out a bestial cry.

Hours later, slightly calmer and sitting on the floor next to Roopmati's bed, Baz opened the notebook and flipped through the delicately handwritten pages. He stopped at the last poem and read aloud, his voice hoarse with tears.

The loved one gives the heart the peace it craves
But, lacking thee, Roopmati knows no peace
For thou art fled! and life holds naught for her
But swift surcease.

He looked out of the window and caught sight of the same bright star he had seen before, aeons ago, it seemed, from Roopmati's pavilion. It flashed once, very bright, just for him.

Epilogue

When Vasant ritu *comes to Malwa, they say the river brings new life to her valley. The meadows and forests burst with such vibrant colours that Holi, the festival of spring, steps back quietly, and is tempted to steal away. But up in the plateau, in Mandu, where the month of Phalgun was once welcomed with the spraying of colours and playing of pranks, the swirling of skirts and the clapping of hands, now, they say, in Mandu, the Goddess of Spring tiptoes quietly from mahal to mahal, looking for something, for someone, in vain. For the monuments lie in darkness, harrowed by sorrow and stained by pain ... the extant tombs of another era. But wait ... hark! Is that a snatch of a distant song on the air? Or is it only the moaning of winds in the ravines of Malwa? Who knows ...*

Glossary

aadaab: a greeting
aaroha: sequence of notes of a raga in ascending order
abbi: now
abbujaan, abbu: father (Urdu)
alaap: the exposition or the opening section of a raga (classical music piece) that sets the mood of the raga.
Allah hafiz: a parting phrase, literally meaning 'may God be your guardian/protector'
amavasya: the first day of the new moon
amma, ammi, ammijaan: mother (in Urdu)
anmol ratan: priceless gem
asana: a length of cloth worn by women that went around the hips and knotted in front
as-salaam-alaikum (also salaam alaikum): greeting among Muslims
asthi: ashes of cremated body

baba: father
badshah-e-jahan: emperor of the world
baithak: sitting room
baoli: a step well
Bazkhani: a style of singing developed by Baz Bahadur
been sitar, been: stringed instrument
beta: son
bhakti rasa: rasa is an emotion expressed by a singer and evoked in the listener by a musical rendition; bhakti rasa is a feeling of devotion to God

burkha: complete veil used by Muslim women, with a netted eyepiece
buttis: motifs/embellishments on clothes

caravansarai: rest houses for travellers
chacha: paternal uncle
chachi: paternal uncle's wife
chalan: an extensive series of note patterns, which summarises the development of a particular raga
chamki: sequin
chogha: a long sleeved coat for men (from the Mughal period)

dadi: paternal grandmother
dhoop: incense to burn, for the essence
Dhrupad: an ancient style of Hindustani classical music; spiritual in nature
dhurrie: woven or knotted floor mat in traditional designs

gati: beat
ghazal: a poetic form of expression originating in Persia and popularised by Sufi poets of the 13th and 14th century; it can be recited or set to music and sung
ghungat: a scarf or dupatta worn covering the head and face
ghungroo: a belt with rows of small metallic bells, usually worn in pairs around the ankles by dancers
gopis: cow girls or milkmaids; in Hindu mythology, Lord Krishna cavorted with gopis as a cowherd

hamam ghar: a traditional bathhouse, where women took oil massages and hot herbal baths
hath: an ancient Indian measure of length
hijra: eunuch
holi: festival of colours to welcome spring
hukkum: a respectful address to one's master/mistress
huzoor: respectful form of address to one's master/mistress

id ka tyauhar: festival of Eid
ittar: traditional perfume

ja: go
jahanpanah: emperor
jal mahal: water palace
jali: lattice screen
jashn: celebration, festival
jhumkas: ear ornament
joothies: traditional ornamental slippers
jowar: a grain
jugalbandi: duet

kachori: a deep fried stuffed savoury snack
kanchuki: a cloth tied across the chest by women
karhai: wok
katar: a sharp, dagger-like weapon
kattha: a paste added to betel leaf while preparing paan
khalajaan: maternal aunt
khariboli: a prestigious dialect that was an important literary medium between the 15th and 19th centuries
khazana: treasure
kund: lake, water body

maalish: massage
maalishwali: masseuse
maika: parental home
mallika: queen
mallika-e-jigr: queen of my heart
milk brother: two men who were breast fed as infants by the same woman
mujra: a dance performed by courtesans
mul, mulmul: fine cotton cloth
mushaira: symposium of poets

nautanki: dramatic behaviour
neevi: a medieval garment of north and central India, it is a length of cloth wound around the waist and gathered in front to fall as pleats to the ankles
Nimadi: language spoken and written in Nimar region of central India

paan daan: an ornate metal box for betel leaves and its accompaniments
paayah-e-takht: capital city
padshah: emperor
pagri: a kind of turban, worn in a particular style
pakad: (in Hindustani music) a musical phrase or set of phrases that contains the melodic theme of the raga, on listening to which, a person who knows the raga, can recognise it
parlok: paradise/the other world
patka: a decorated/embellished sash worn by men in Mughal times
peher: the three-hour period
pice: old Indian coin
prasad: an offering to gods

ratna: gems
raunaq: buzz
riyaz: practice
roos: Russian
ruk: stop

safa: an elaborately tied turban
sahibaah: lady
salaki: a tree native to the Malwa region, from which frankincense is obtained
sandhyakaal: evening time
sarangi: a stringed musical instrument played with a bow
sasural: husband's home/in-law's home
senapati: commander of the forces, in a Hindu kingdom
seva: service

shahi mahal: palace for royal guests
shahzadi: queen
sharara: a pair of loose pleated trousers worn by women, typically with a kameez and dupatta
shauhar: husband
shringara rasa: rasa is an emotion expressed by a singer and evoked in the listener by a musical rendition; shringara rasa expresses romantic love, attraction, lovers' interactions and mystical experiences
shruti: melody
sipahsalar: a commander of forces in the Mughal army
sur: musical notes

taal: beat
tabeli mahal: building where horses were stabled
tailapatra: eucalyptus tree, native to Malwa region
thaal: plate
til: sesame seed

ubtan: a paste made of herbs rubbed on the body while bathing
ushakaal: early morning
ustad-e-mosiqui: maestro of music
uttariya: a shawl-like cloth worn to cover the kanchuki

vasant ritu: spring season

walaikum salaam: the appropriate reply to the greeting as-salaam-alaikum
wazir-e-azam: prime minister

yug: epoch
zafrani zarda: chewing tobacco cut up and mixed with saffron strands and spices
zananakhana: living quarters reserved for wives and concubines and female relatives in a Muslim household

Acknowledgements

Writing historical fiction is always an aggregate of unrelenting research, imagination riding a time machine and expert inputs. I have tried to be meticulous with the first, been adventurous with the second and very fortunate with the third.

I have quoted from the poems of both Baz and Roopmati. On the works of Baz, my source is sketchy. I have taken the liberty to use the verses and their translation as they are from the paper by Dr Abdul Halim, MA, PhD, Professor and Head of the Department of History, University of Dacca.

Roopmati's poems on pages 181, 191, 232 and 251 are from L.C. Crump's *The Lady of the Lotus*, a translation of the Persian work by Ahmad-ul-Umari (1599). It records the love story of Roopmati and Baz Bahadur and includes 26 poems written by Roopmati herself. Other verses attributed to her have been imagined by me.

I take this opportunity to thank my erudite friends and critics Ashvani Kumar Sachdev and Vidya Ramachandran, who took the time to read and give me invaluable suggestions on the first draft, and my editor, Keerti Ramachandra, who vetted the manuscript to reach its final form.

A big thank you also to my family and close friends, always behind me, always believing in me.

About the Author

Malathi Ramachandran is the author of three novels; this is her fourth. A Masters in Mass Communications, she dabbled with writing middles, features and travelogues before finding her forte in fiction. Her short stories have been published in magazines and anthologies. Her passion for the history and cultural heritage of the country takes her to little known towns and hamlets where she often finds stories to share.

'The epiphany in writing historical fiction,' she says, 'is in knowing that human thoughts, feelings, emotions never change, no matter how many centuries pass. Love and loss are always the same.'

Malathi's last book in this genre, *The Legend of Kuldhara*, recreates the story of an abandoned village in the Rajasthan desert and the lives that were changed forever one fateful night.

She invites interaction at malathiram56@gmail.com

